SIDE QUEST

SIDE

QUEST

A VISUAL HISTORY OF ROLEPLAYING GAMES

STEENZ · **SAMUEL SATTIN**

INTERIOR FLATS BY AISHWARYA TANDON

▼ VERSIFY

Imprints of HarperCollinsPublishers

HARPER alley

A NOTE FROM THE AUTHORS

While our research is thorough, we have by no means created a decisive history of roleplaying games. In fact, if this book can be claimed to be decisive in any way, it should be only that it encourages readers to discover what they find interesting or exciting about the phenomenon. Additionally, we have used a variety of references for the games, people, and places in this book. But considering there was no photography before the 1800s, we did our best based on what we had available: writings, paintings, ceramics, drawings, and illustrated portraits. Thank you for understanding!

Versify is an imprint of HarperCollins Publishers.
HarperAlley is an imprint of HarperCollins Publishers.

Side Quest
Text copyright © 2024 by Samuel Sattin
Illustrations copyright © 2024 by Christina A. Stewart
All rights reserved. Manufactured in Bosnia and Herzegovina.

Library of Congress Control Number: 2023943945
ISBN 978-0-35-861636-8 — ISBN 978-0-35-861637-5 (pbk.)

The artist used Clip Studio Paint to create the digital illustrations for this book.
Typography by Joe Merkel
Flatted by Aishwarya Tandon
Interior Lettering by D.C. Hopkins
24 25 26 27 28   GPS   10 9 8 7 6 5 4 3 2 1
First Edition

For Dani, my first Dungeon Master
—**STEENZ**

To the owners of Attactix and their ample shelves
filled with *Dragon* magazine
—**SAMUEL**

Contents

Part One

BEGINNING THE ADVENTURE

LUMINA CITY
DESTINATION: MAGRAK'S PYLON

SEEMS A LITTLE QUIET FOR LUMINA CITY, DON'T YOU THINK, ASR-33?

NO NEED FOR FORMALITIES, GARBOON.

CALL ME 33.

BUT YES. THIS QUIET IS UNUSUAL.

UNUSUAL IN MY BOOK MEANS DANGEROUS.

I DIDN'T KNOW YOU READ BOOKS, GARBOON.

I HAVE READ EXACTLY ONE BOOK.

BAZFARK, MOORFUS, WHAT DO YOU SEE? CLEAR SAILING?

I'LL CHECK, CAPTAIN!

HMM...

JUST A COUPLE OF PASSENGER CONVOYS. NOTHING TO WORRY ABOUT.

THOSE AREN'T PASSENGER CONVOYS, BAZFARK. CHECK AGAIN!

BZZT

IGUADARS!

HOW DID THEY GET THROUGH LUMINA'S VEIL?

MUST HAVE FOUND A TECHNOMANCER.

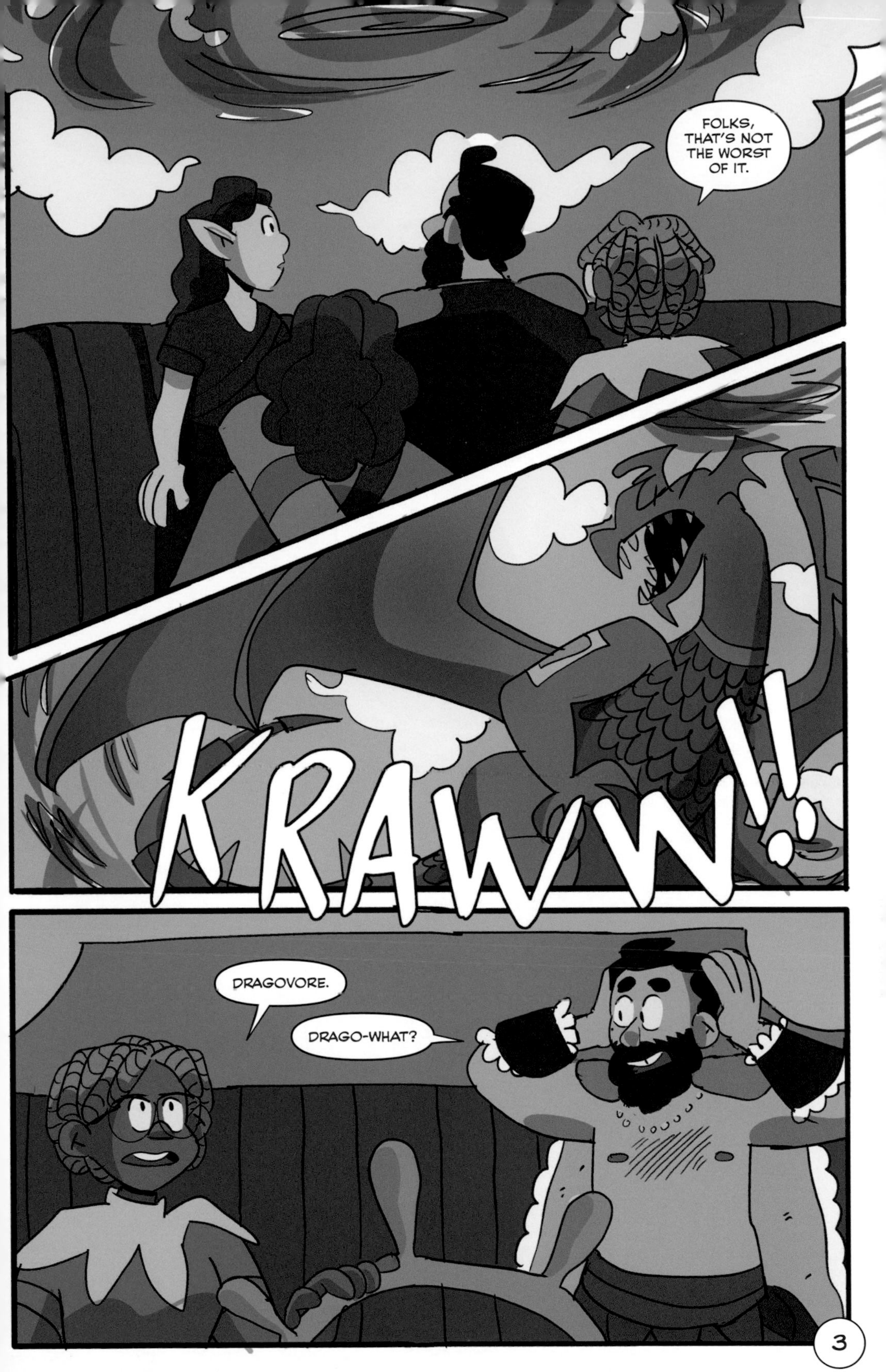
FOLKS, THAT'S NOT THE WORST OF IT.
KRAWW!!
DRAGOVORE.
DRAGO-WHAT?

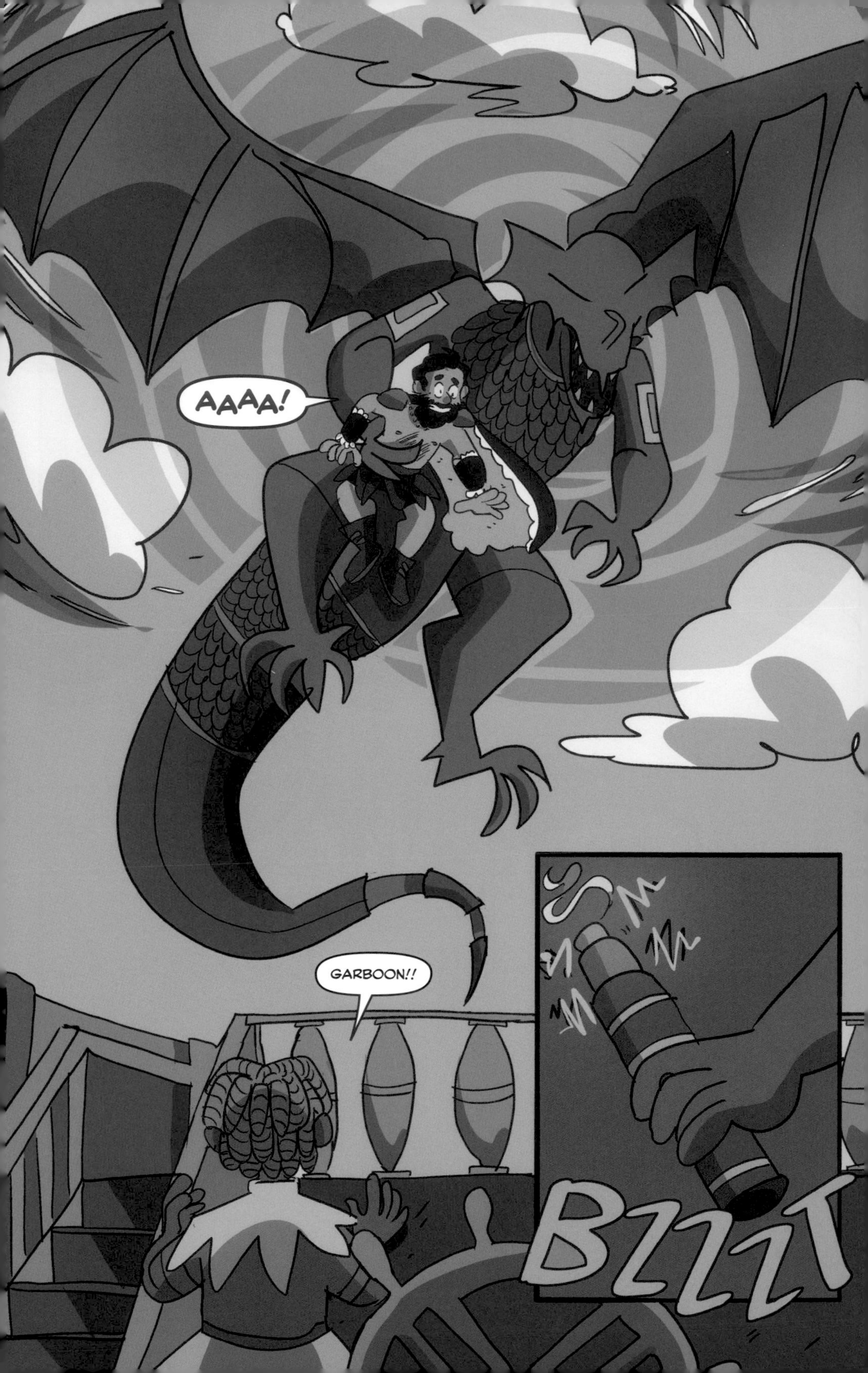
AAAA!
GARBOON!!
BZZZT

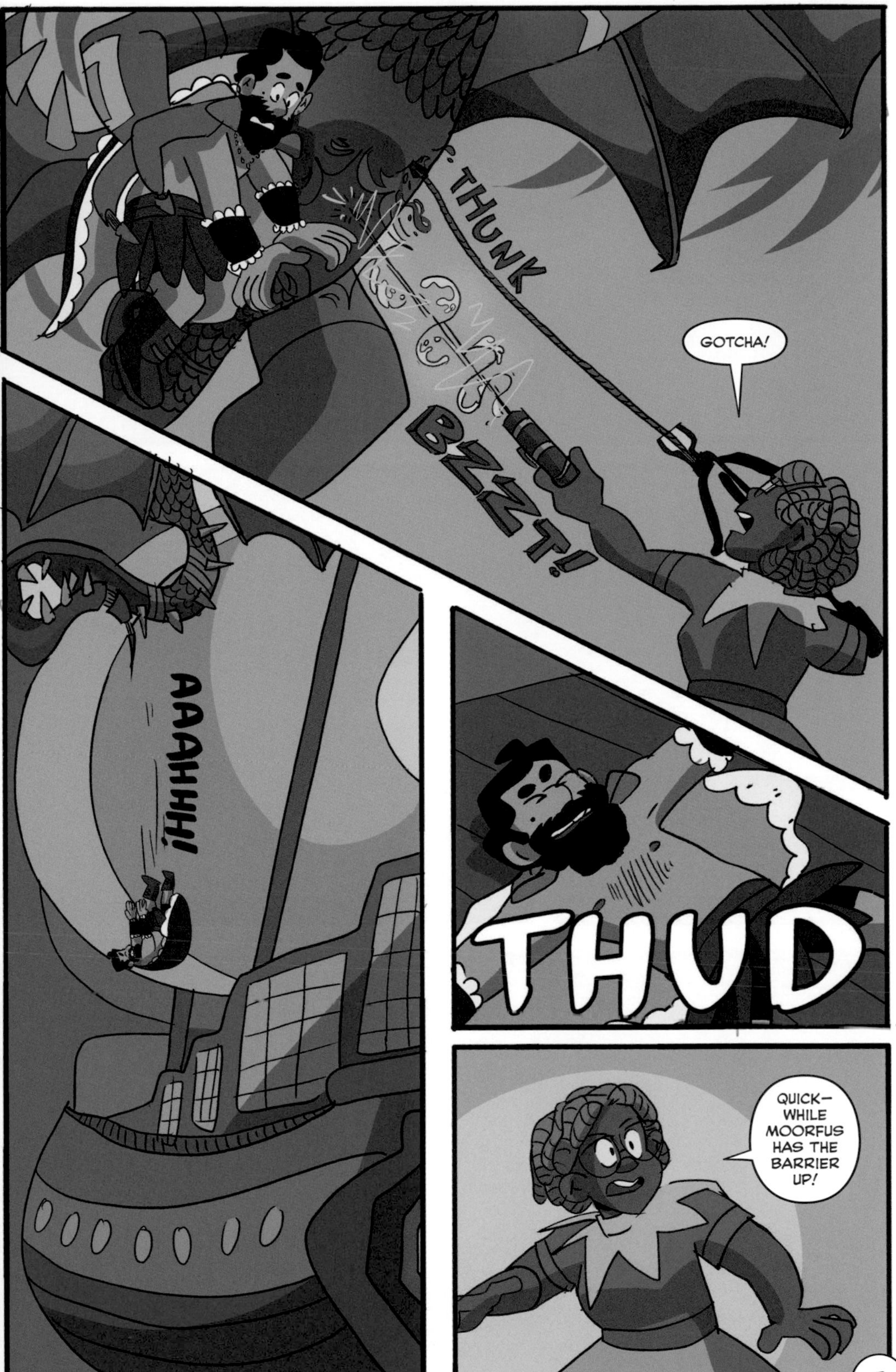
THUNK
BZZZT!
GOTCHA!
AAAAHHH!
THUD
QUICK—WHILE MOORFUS HAS THE BARRIER UP!

THIS BARRIER ISN'T GOING TO LAST MUCH LONGER!

I'M GOING TO GIVE YOU SOME WINGS, GARBOON!

HOLD STILL.

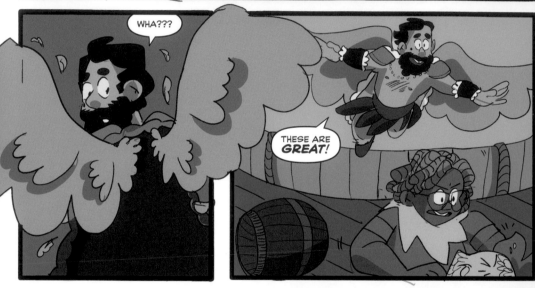

WHA???

THESE ARE *GREAT!*

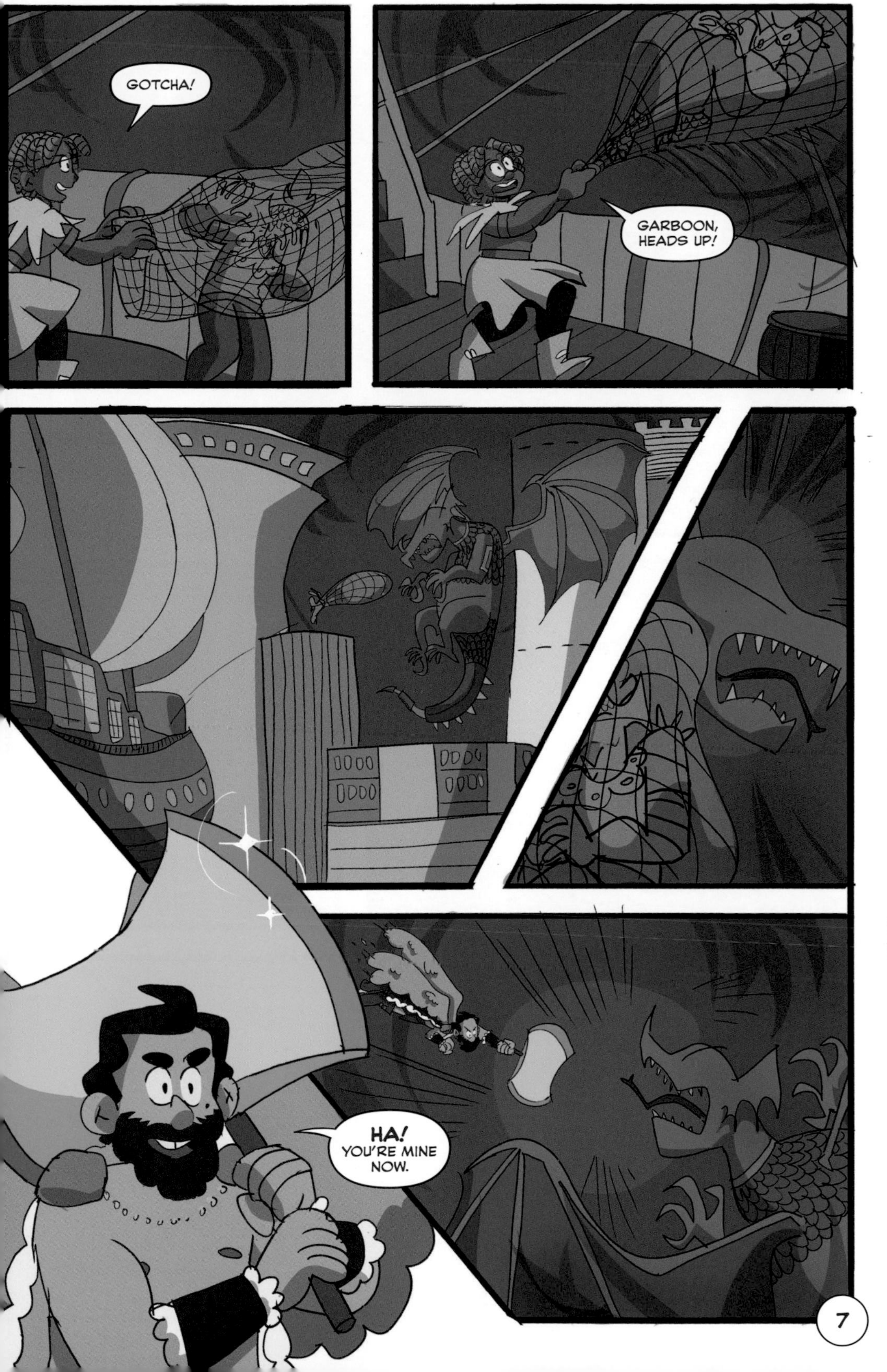
GOTCHA!
GARBOON, HEADS UP!
HA! YOU'RE MINE NOW.

SPLAT

SPLAT

KA FOO M

WE DID IT!

OF COURSE WE DID.

HIGH FIVE

UH, GUYS?

THIS ISN'T GOOD.

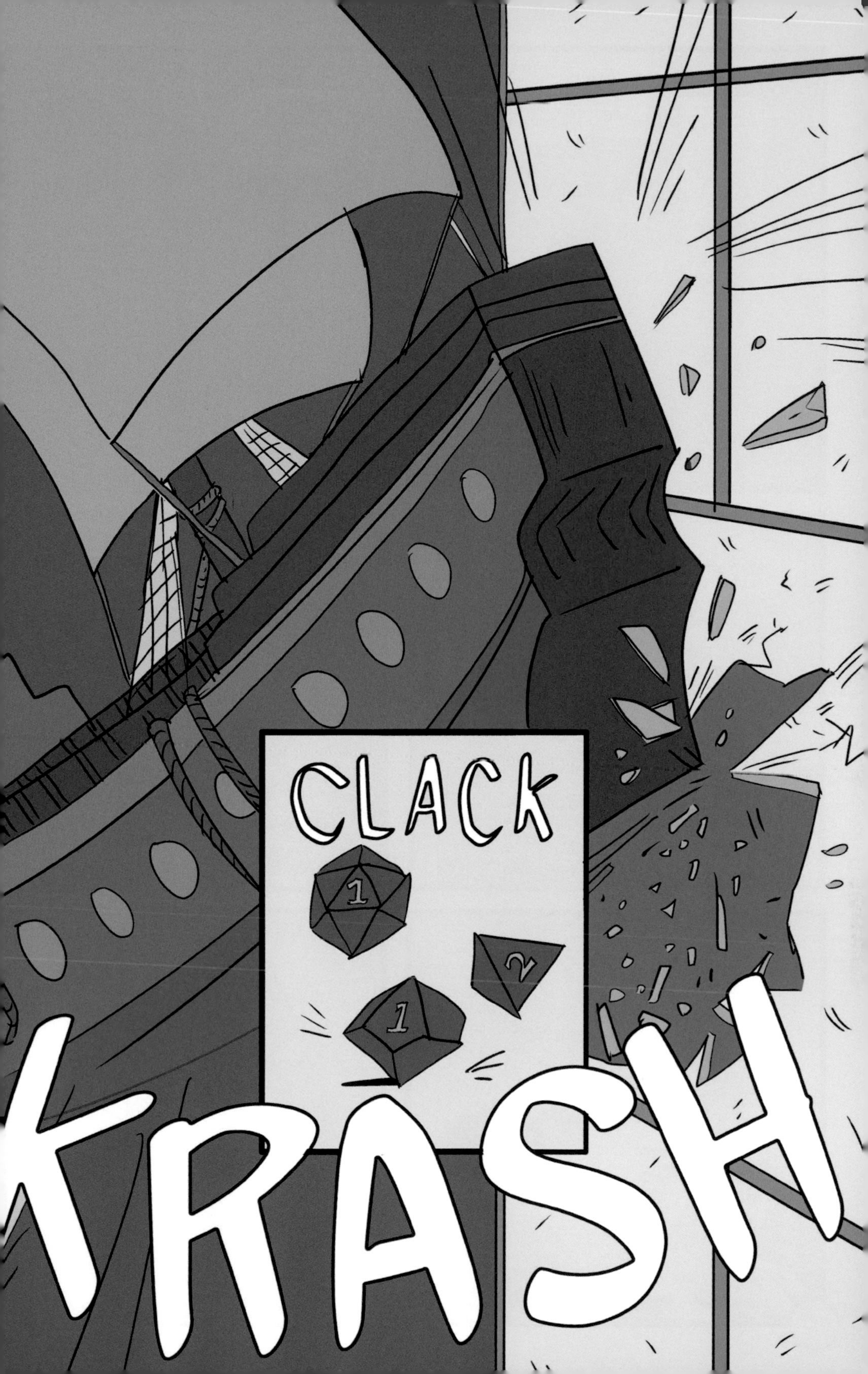
CLACK
1
2
1
KRASH

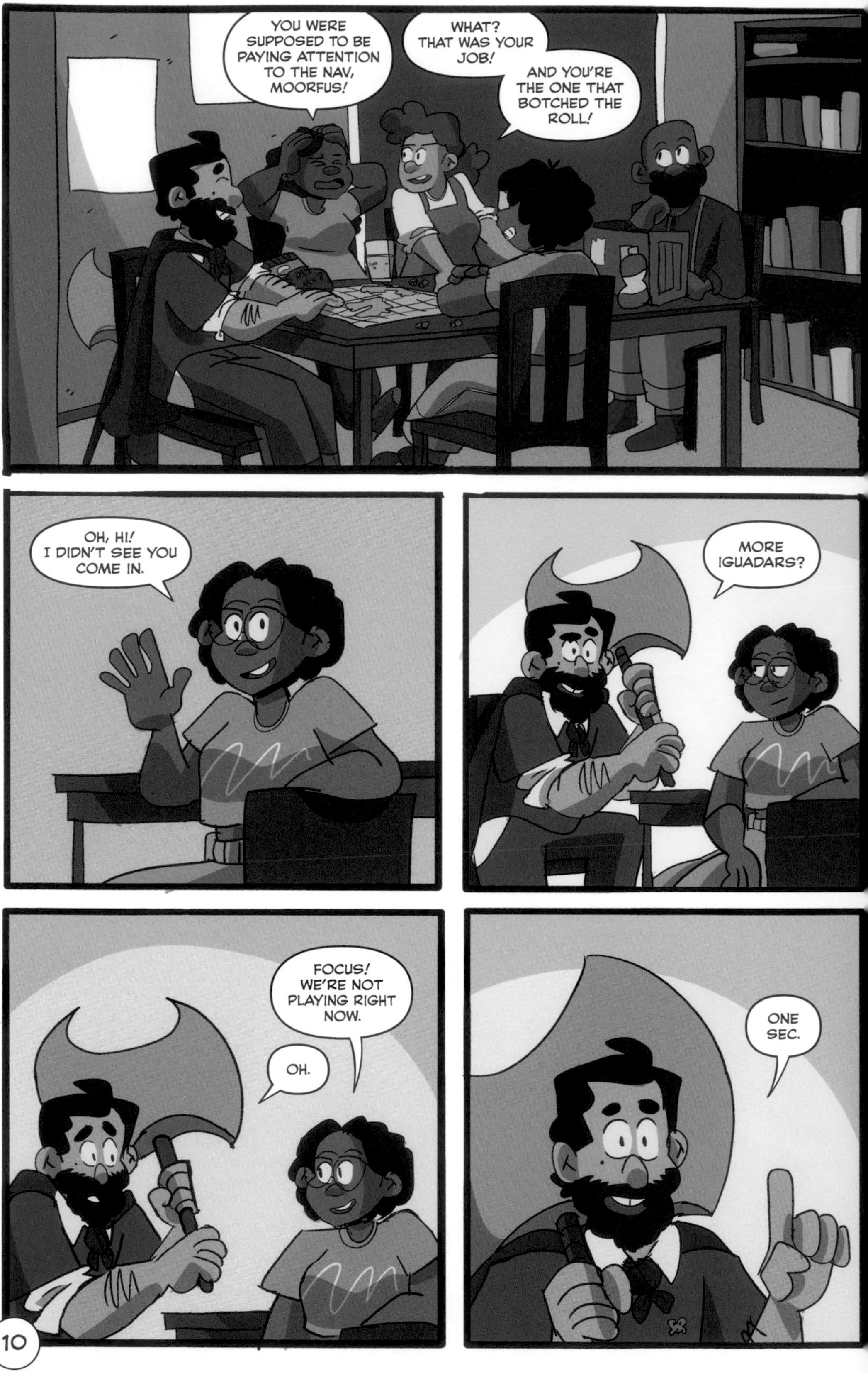
YOU WERE SUPPOSED TO BE PAYING ATTENTION TO THE NAV, MOORFUS!
WHAT? THAT WAS YOUR JOB!
AND YOU'RE THE ONE THAT BOTCHED THE ROLL!
OH, HI! I DIDN'T SEE YOU COME IN.
MORE IGUADARS?
OH.
FOCUS! WE'RE NOT PLAYING RIGHT NOW.
ONE SEC.

ANYWAY, WELCOME!

SAM, THESE GOOD PEOPLE ARE HERE TO LEARN ABOUT ROLEPLAYING GAMES.

RIGHT— THAT'S TODAY!

WELCOME TO A HISTORY OF TTRPGS! THANK YOU FOR COMING!

AS YOU CAN SEE, WE WERE IMMERSED IN A GAME OURSELVES.

YES! WE WERE PLAYING A TABLETOP ROLEPLAYING GAME, OR TTRPG FOR SHORT.

THESE GAMES CAN PRACTICALLY TRANSPORT YOU TO A DIFFERENT UNIVERSE.

WELL, NOT IN THE WAY THAT YOU'D LOSE TRACK OF REALITY, OF COURSE!

NO WAY. IN FACT, IDEAS LIKE THAT HAVE LED TO NEGATIVE STEREOTYPES.

SOME RELIGIOUS CONSERVATIVES CLAIMED TTRPGS CONTAINED WITCHCRAFT.

BUT WITH ROLEPLAYING GAMES, A ROBUST IMAGINATION COMES IN HANDY.

ALONGSIDE A SET OF **DICE**, **CHARACTER SHEETS**, SCRAP PAPER, AND DEPENDING ON WHAT YOU'RE PLAYING, A COLLECTION OF MANUALS...

YOU CAN CREATE AND INHABIT NEW UNIVERSES!

BUT FOR THOSE OF US WHO DON'T KNOW MUCH ABOUT THESE GAMES, AND EVEN FOR THOSE OF YOU WHO DO...

WE'RE EXCITED TO TAKE YOU ON THIS JOURNEY THROUGH TIME, EXPERIENCE, AND IMAGINATION TO EXPLORE THE HISTORY OF TABLETOP ROLEPLAYING GAMES!

ARE YOU PREPARED TO EMBARK ON A QUEST ACROSS THE SANDS OF SPACE AND TIME?

INTO THE ORIGINS OF WHAT MAKES US TELL STORIES?

AND EVEN MORE SO, WHAT MAKES US WANT TO LIVE *INSIDE* THOSE STORIES?

BEFORE WE DIVE IN, SHOULDN'T WE GIVE THESE FOLKS A DEFINITION?

A DEFINITION?

OF TTRPGS?

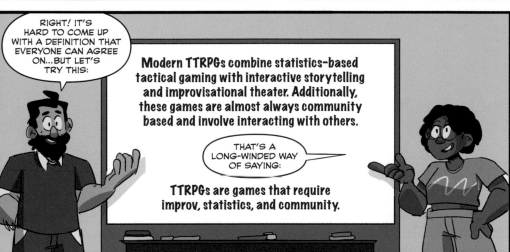

RIGHT! IT'S HARD TO COME UP WITH A DEFINITION THAT EVERYONE CAN AGREE ON...BUT LET'S TRY THIS:

Modern TTRPGs combine statistics-based tactical gaming with interactive storytelling and improvisational theater. Additionally, these games are almost always community based and involve interacting with others.

THAT'S A LONG-WINDED WAY OF SAYING:

TTRPGs are games that require improv, statistics, and community.

BUT DON'T WORRY, WE'RE NOT STOPPING THERE. IN FACT, WE'RE JUST STARTING!

LET'S HAVE A LOOK AT SOME OF THE THINGS YOU NEED TO PLAY A MODERN TTRPG.

LET'S SEE HERE...

13

TO BEGIN WITH, YOU'LL NEED SOME KIND OF FLAT SURFACE, LIKE A TABLE.

WHY? BECAUSE OF...

DICE. A LOT OF TTRPGS USE THEM.

AND THEY NEED TO BE ABLE TO ROLL.

TRADITIONAL TTRPGS USE POLYHEDRAL DICE, WHICH JUST MEANS THEY ARE THREE-DIMENSIONAL SHAPES WITH EQUAL SIDES.

YOU MIGHT SEE THIS ONE A LOT IN PARTICULAR.

20-SIDED (D20)

4-SIDED (D4)

6-SIDED (D6)
THE MOST COMMON TYPE OF DIE IN POPULAR BOARD GAMES

8-SIDED (D8)

10-SIDED (D10)

12-SIDED (D12)

THE TWENTY-SIDED DIE (D20) BECAME POPULAR IN TTRPGS BECAUSE OF ITS ABILITY TO INCREASE PROBABILITY FOR OUTCOMES.

BUT MANY OTHER KINDS EXIST!

MOST TTRPGS HAVE RULE SYSTEMS AND TAILOR-MADE **CAMPAIGN** MODULES.

MANY REQUIRE A GUIDE FOR PLAYERS AND A GUIDE FOR **GAME MASTERS**, OR GMS (DUNGEON MASTERS, OR DMS, IN **DUNGEONS & DRAGONS**).

OR IN SOME CIRCUMSTANCES: REFEREES!

WITH MOST TTRPGS, YOU'LL HAVE A CHARACTER SHEET THAT CONTAINS ATTRIBUTES OF THE CHARACTER YOU'LL BE PLAYING.

THESE ATTRIBUTES CAN VARY BASED ON THE GAME, BUT THEY ARE MOST OFTEN ACCOMPANIED BY NUMERICAL STATISTICS TO BE USED DURING GAME PLAY.

EXPERIENCE

ARMOR CLASS

HIT POINTS

ABILITIES

SAVING THROWS

STRENGTH

INTELLIGENCE

WISDOM

DEXTERITY

CONSTITUTION

POISON or DEA[TH]

MAGIC WAND

PARALYSIS

DRAGON BREATH

SPELLS

Weapon in hand (DMG)

6 5 4 3 2 1 0 -1

PEOPLE OFTEN ILLUSTRATE THEIR CHARACTERS IF THEY CAN.

AND DEPENDING ON WHAT GAME YOU'RE PLAYING, **MINI-FIGURINES** CAN BE USED TO REPRESENT NOT ONLY THEM BUT OTHER CHARACTERS AND CREATURES.

A COUPLE OF WRITING IMPLEMENTS, A WAY FOR THE GM TO CONCEAL THE ADVENTURE, AND A GOOD SOURCE OF LIGHT, AND YOU CAN PLAY MOST ANY TTRPG IN EXISTENCE!

A LOT OF PEOPLE GREW UP PLAYING TTRPGS.

I PERSONALLY DIDN'T KNOW MUCH ABOUT THEM UNTIL I WAS OLDER.

EVERYONE HAS A DIFFERENT ENTRY POINT.

I STARTED PLAYING TOWARD THE END OF MIDDLE SCHOOL, SINCE I HAD A FEW FRIENDS WHO WANTED TO GIVE IT A TRY.

EVEN IF YOU DON'T GROW UP WITH TTRPGS, YOU CAN BE READY FOR THEM FROM A VERY YOUNG AGE.

YOU'RE RIGHT!

KIDS ENGAGE IN IMAGINATIVE PLAY LONG BEFORE THEY ENCOUNTER POLYHEDRAL DICE, WHICH IS A HUGE PART OF WHAT MAKES TTRPGS WORK.

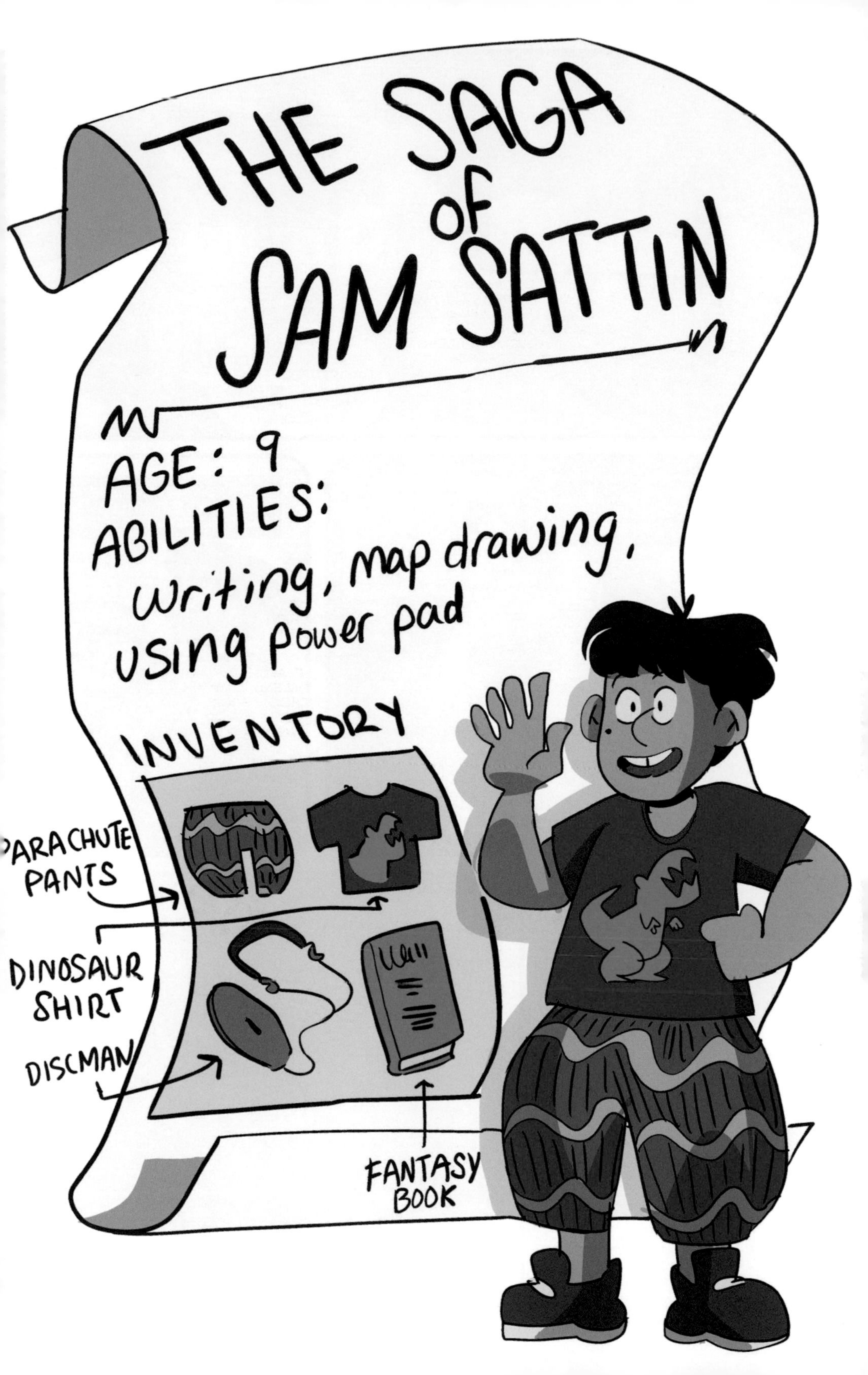
THE SAGA of SAM SATTIN
AGE: 9
ABILITIES:
writing, map drawing,
using power pad
INVENTORY
PARACHUTE PANTS
DINOSAUR SHIRT
DISCMAN
FANTASY BOOK

IT'S A BEAUTIFUL SUMMER DAY. PERFECT FOR A GAME OF TEENAGE MUTANT NINJA TURTLES.

Sam

THERE AREN'T ANY SET RULES IN THIS GAME—EXCEPT, OF COURSE, TO PRETEND.

WATCH OUT, DONATELLO!

I'D WANTED TO BE LEONARDO, BUT KIM CALLED IT FIRST. SO DONATELLO IT WAS!

BUT SINCE NONE OF US HAD A BO STAFF, I WIELDED AN ALUMINUM BASEBALL BAT.

MORE ON THAT SHORTLY...

IN THE ACT OF PRETENDING, WE WERE TRANSPORTED FROM THE SUBURBS OF ARAPAHOE COUNTY, COLORADO, TO THE MUTAGEN-SOAKED STREETS OF EARLY '90S NEW YORK CITY.

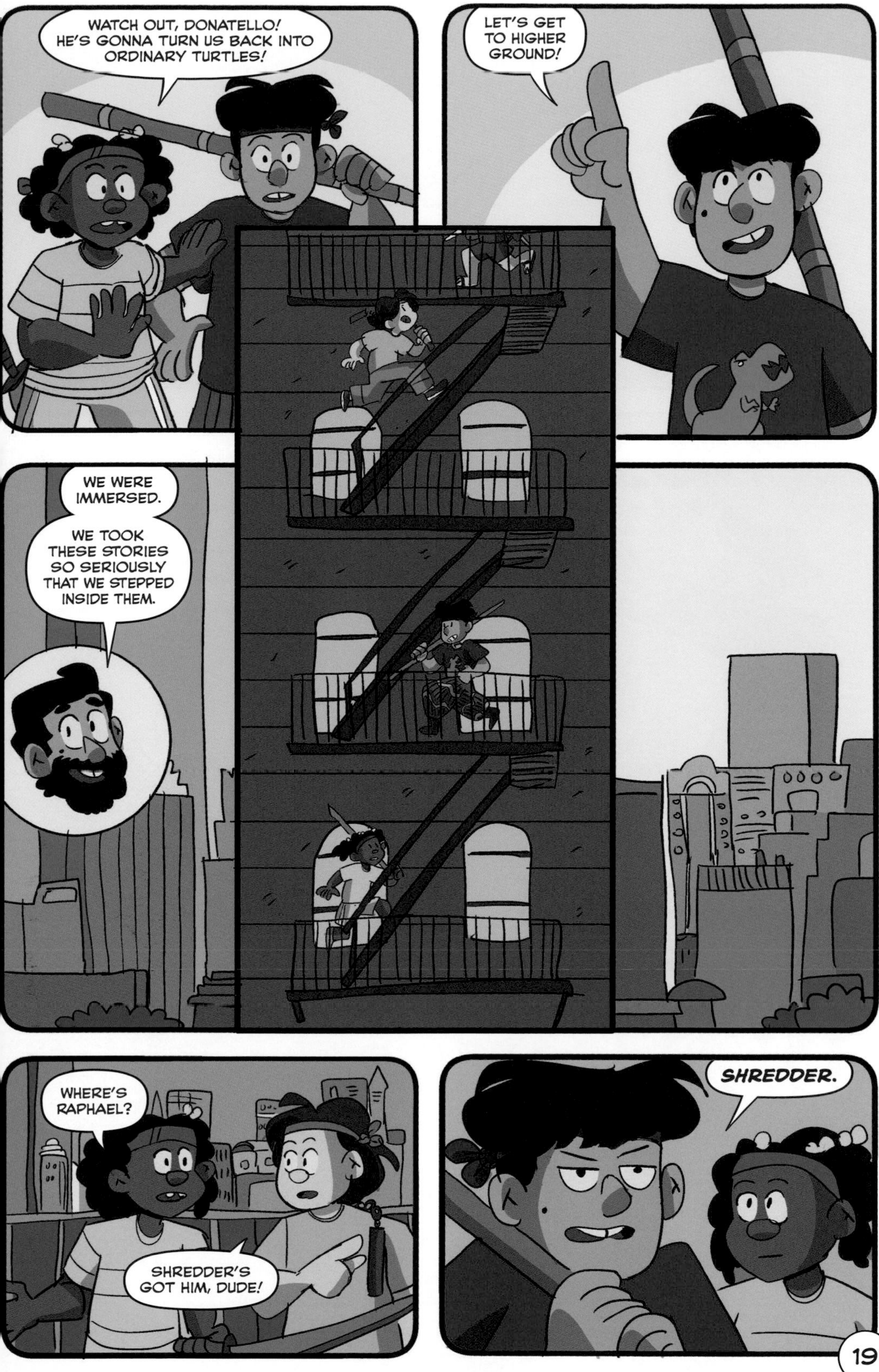
WATCH OUT, DONATELLO! HE'S GONNA TURN US BACK INTO ORDINARY TURTLES!
LET'S GET TO HIGHER GROUND!
WE WERE IMMERSED.
WE TOOK THESE STORIES SO SERIOUSLY THAT WE STEPPED INSIDE THEM.
WHERE'S RAPHAEL?
SHREDDER'S GOT HIM, DUDE!
SHREDDER.

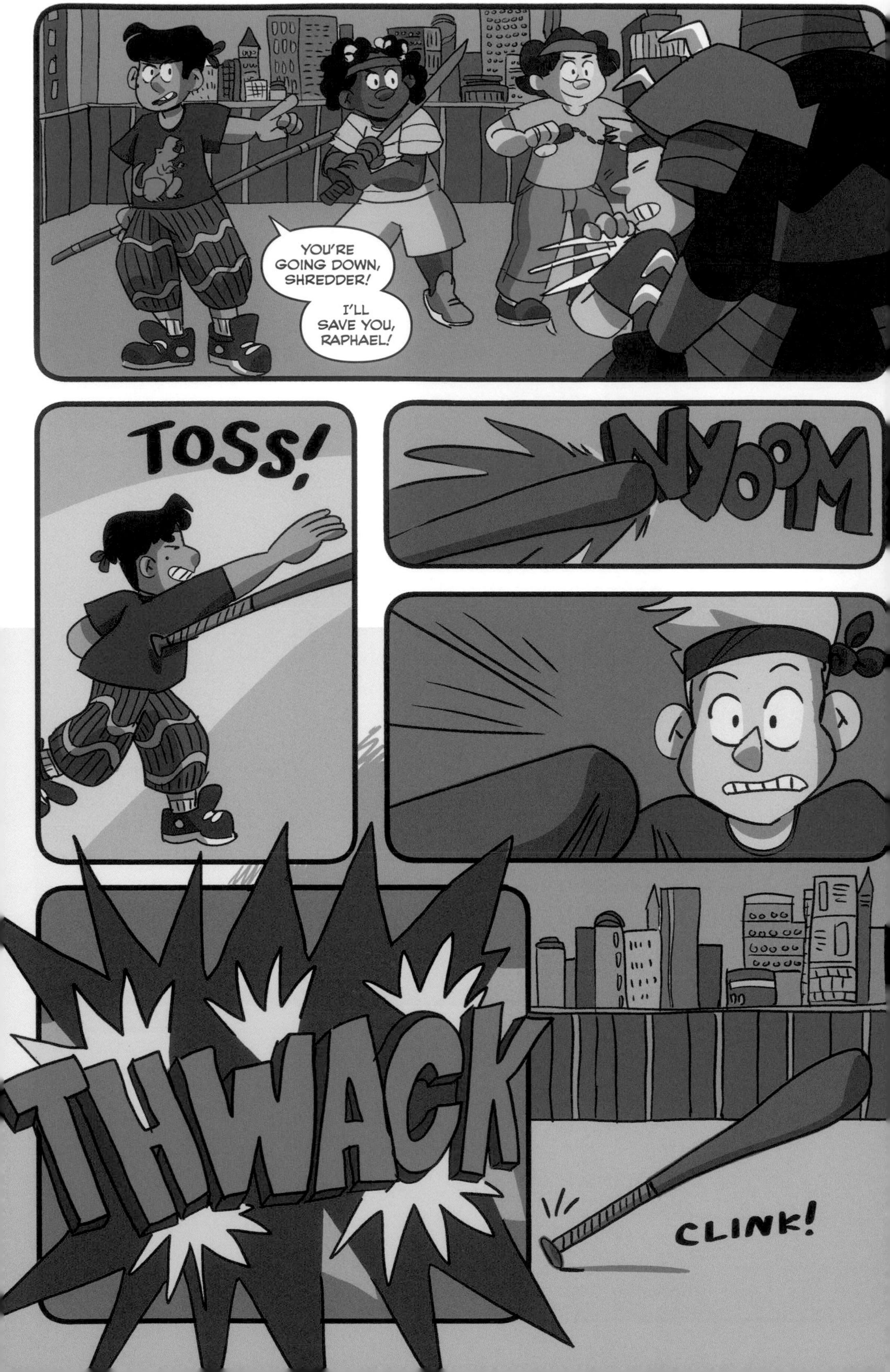
YOU'RE GOING DOWN, SHREDDER!
I'LL SAVE YOU, RAPHAEL!
TOSS!
NYOOM
THWACK
CLINK!

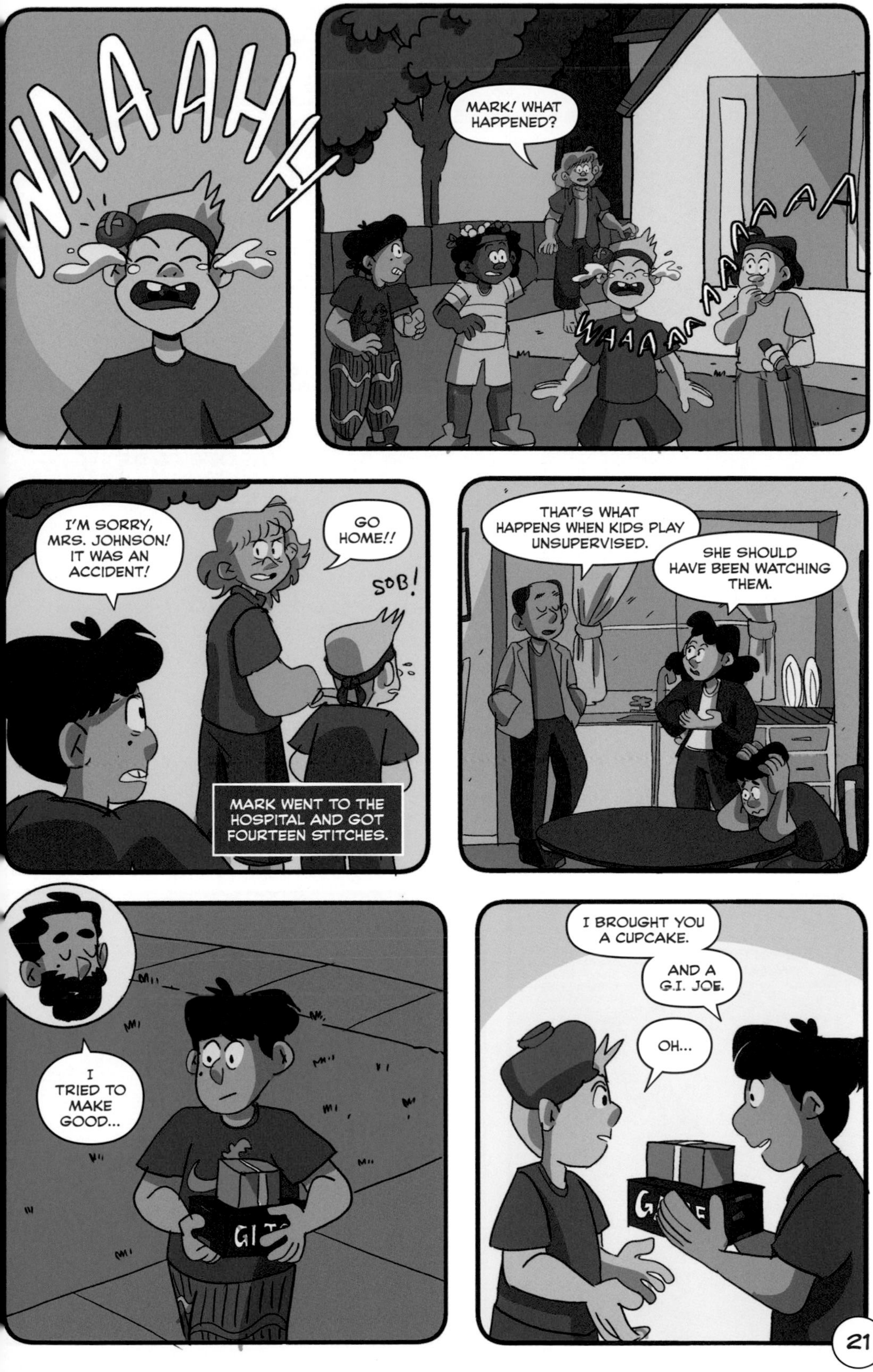
WAAAHH
MARK! WHAT HAPPENED?
WAAAAAAAAAAAA
I'M SORRY, MRS. JOHNSON! IT WAS AN ACCIDENT!
GO HOME!!
SOB!
MARK WENT TO THE HOSPITAL AND GOT FOURTEEN STITCHES.
THAT'S WHAT HAPPENS WHEN KIDS PLAY UNSUPERVISED.
SHE SHOULD HAVE BEEN WATCHING THEM.
I TRIED TO MAKE GOOD...
I BROUGHT YOU A CUPCAKE.
AND A G.I. JOE.
OH...

BUT NO CUPCAKE WAS SWEET ENOUGH TO UNSOUR MY DEED.

WE DON'T WANT YOU PLAYING WITH MARK ANYMORE.

PLAYING PRETEND LED TO EXILE.

IMAGINATION AND REAL LIFE BECAME BLURRED FOR A MOMENT.

YEESH. POOR MARK.

I DON'T REMEMBER HURTING HIM THAT BAD.

PRETEND PLAY IS A MAJOR WAY THAT HUMANS DISCOVER HOW TO INTERACT WITH OTHERS AND THE WORLD AROUND THEM.

WHETHER IT'S PIRATES, COWBOYS, OR NINJA TURTLES, PEOPLE INSERT THEMSELVES INTO IMAGINARY ROLES TO INHABIT THE STORIES THEY LOVE.

MAYBE ONE OF THE REASONS TTRPGS APPEAL TO ADULTS IS THAT PRETEND PLAY IS CONSIDERED SOMETHING ONLY KIDS SHOULD DO.

WE'RE EXPECTED TO OUTGROW THE REALM OF MAKE-BELIEVE.

WHICH IS KINDA A WACK WAY TO THINK!

SO WACK!

BUT THE POPULARITY OF ALL DIFFERENT KINDS OF GAMES ACROSS ADULT DEMOGRAPHICS DEMONSTRATES OTHERWISE.

THERE ARE TONS OF DIGITAL RPGS IN VIDEO GAMES!

BUT WE'RE NOT GOING TO CONCENTRATE ON THOSE.

BESIDES, NONE OF THEM WOULD HAVE EXISTED AT ALL WITHOUT TABLETOP GAMES.

VIDEO GAMES

KIDS TOYS

SPEAKING OF DIFFERENT KINDS OF RPGS, THEY CAN BE THOUGHT TO FALL INTO THREE CATEGORIES: TABLETOP, LIVE ACTION ROLEPLAYING (**LARPING**), AND ELECTRONIC (VIDEO GAMES).

BUT MY INTRODUCTION TO GAMING WAS MORE TRADITIONAL.

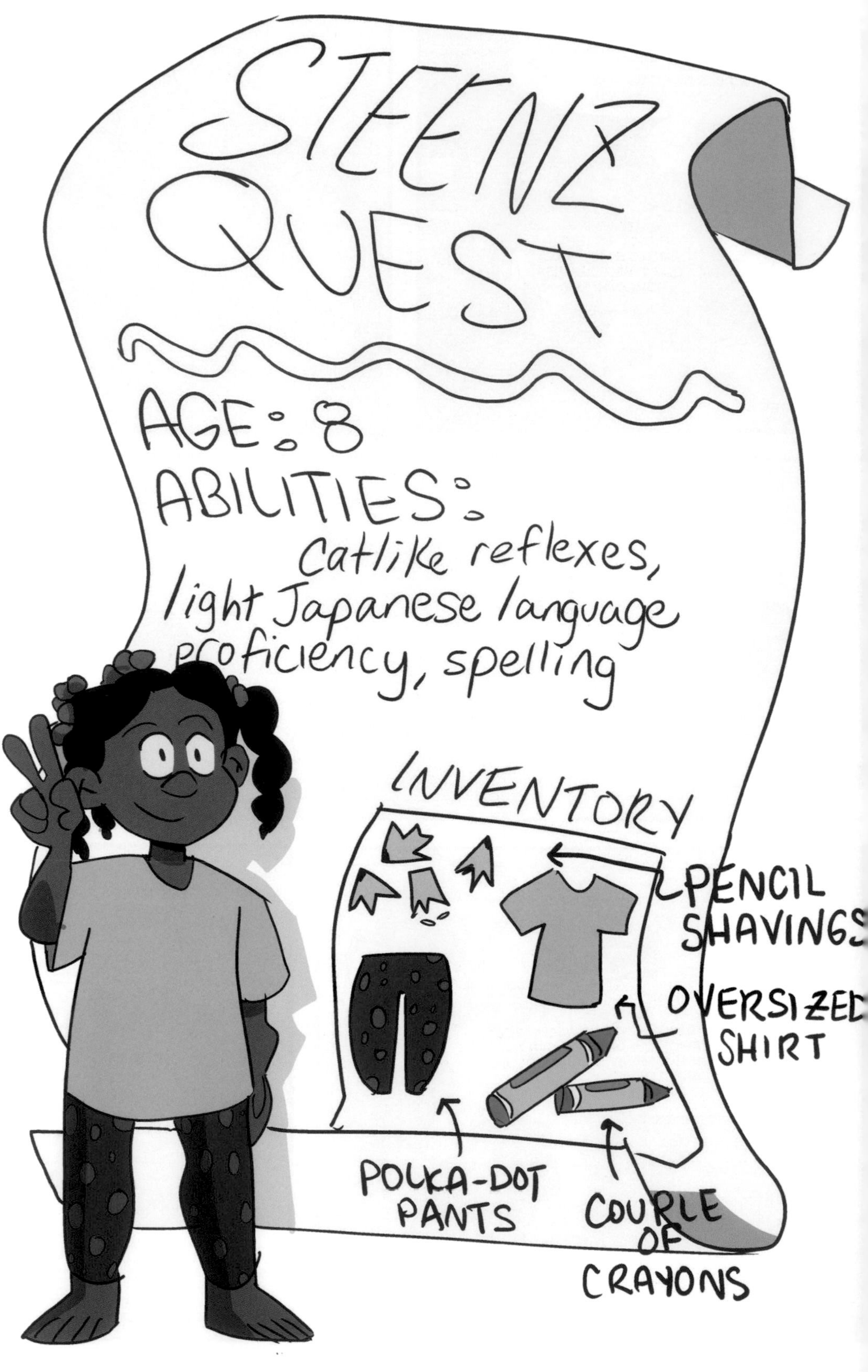
STEENZ QUEST
AGE: 8
ABILITIES:
catlike reflexes, light Japanese language proficiency, spelling
INVENTORY
PENCIL SHAVINGS
OVERSIZED SHIRT
POLKA-DOT PANTS
COUPLE OF CRAYONS

MY TWIN SISTER, CELESTE, AND I SPENT ALL OUR TIME TOGETHER GROWING UP.

BUT I *JUST* READ THE RULES, CELESTE!

Steenz
I BECAME ATTACHED TO FOLLOWING RULES.

AND WE'RE *NOT SUPPOSED* TO KEEP ROLLING.

BUT WE'VE BEEN PLAYING THIS WAY *FOREVER*. WHY DO WE HAVE TO CHANGE IT NOW?

UNLIKE MY TWIN SISTER.

WATCH. IF WE PLAY IT THE WAY THE RULES SAY, THEN THE GAME WON'T GO SO FAST.

NO, I LIKE IT THE OTHER WAY!

BUT WHY CAN'T WE DO IT THE RIGHT WAY?

BECAUSE WE ALREADY DID AND I DIDN'T LIKE IT!

I DON'T WANT TO ARGUE. AND I DEFINITELY DON'T WANT TO PLAY ANYMORE.

WHA

COME BACK AND PLAY WITH ME!!

I DON'T WANT TO!!

QUIT YELLIN' ACROSS THE HOUSE!

I JUST DIDN'T UNDERSTAND HOW SOMEONE COULD PLAY A GAME WRONG. AND *ON PURPOSE*...

...BUT I ALSO DIDN'T CONSIDER **WHY** CELESTE WANTED TO PLAY THE GAME HER OWN WAY.

SNIFF!

WHEN YOU PLAY A GAME LIKE SHE DID, YOU ENTER YOUR OWN WORLD.

YOU ALTER EXISTING RULES SO THE GAME MAKES SENSE TO **YOU**, REGARDLESS OF WHETHER IT'S CORRECT OR NOT.

STILL, PLAYING A GAME ACCORDING TO THE RULES SEEMED LIKE THE ONLY WAY FOR ME. SO MUCH SO, I BECAME INTERESTED IN THE DIRECTIONS THEMSELVES.

I STUDIED THE DIRECTIONS FOR CANDY LAND, CHUTES AND LADDERS, MONOPOLY...

I DIDN'T REALIZE THIS UNTIL LATER IN LIFE...

...BUT I WANTED TO ABIDE BY THE RULES SO I COULD TEACH NEW PLAYERS HOW TO PLAY.

MONOPOLY

SO **THEY** WOULDN'T HAVE TO GO THROUGH THE TEDIOUS TASK OF READING THROUGH THE DIRECTIONS.

I WANTED TO HELP OTHERS HAVE FUN.

SO AS YOU CAN SEE, I'M INTO RULES.

GOTTA HAVE 'EM!

RULES ARE AN IMPORTANT PART OF WHAT MAKES TTRPGS NOT JUST PLAYABLE BUT ACCESSIBLE TO PEOPLE ACROSS VARIOUS DEMOGRAPHICS.

THEY CREATE STANDARDS.

HOW TO PLAY

TO DETERMINE AN ACTION'S SUCCESS, PERFORM THESE ACTIONS:

1. ROLL D100, ADD THE ABILITY SCORE, AND THEN USE THIS RESULT TO DETERMINE WHICH DIE TO ROLL IN STEP 2. ON A RESULT OF 1-20 ROLL A D4; ON 21-40 ROLL D6; ON 41-60 ROLL D8; 61-80: D10; 81-100: D12. TO COPE WITH RESULTS HIGHER THAN 100, CREATE A HOUSE RULE FOR THIS HOUSE RULE.

2. ROLL THE DIE DETERMINED IN STEP 1 AND MULTIPLY THE NUMBER BY THE ATTRI... ...RESULT BECOMES THE ...CESS.

3. RO... ...RESULT IS LESS THAN ...E PROBABILITY FR... ...SUCCEED!

BUT SOMETIMES, IF THESE RULES ARE UNCLEAR OR OVERLY COMPLICATED, THEY CAN GET IN THE WAY OF THE FUN AND HAVE TO BE REVISED OR SET ASIDE.

BUT WHAT WAS BEFORE POLYHEDRAL DICE, EXPERIENCE POINTS, AND TREASURE CHESTS? SHOULD WE GET INTO THE EARLY ORIGINS OF ROLEPLAYING?

WE DEFINITELY SHOULD!

OH NO.

LET'S GET THIS THING WORKING.

IS THAT THE "TIME MACHINE" YOU FOUND BEHIND THE SUPERMARKET?

UNIMPORTANT! LET'S HEAD BACK BEFORE 1974, WHEN SOME NERDY WISCONSINITES RELEASED DUNGEONS & DRAGONS...

TO EXPLORE THE ROOTS OF INTERACTIVE, IMAGINATIVE PLAY.

THERE'S NO WAY THAT'S GOING TO WO—

BZZHH

Part Two

BOOKS
OF
LORE

WE MADE IT! WHERE SHOULD WE PARK?

THE ORIGINS OF IMAGINATIVE PLAY CAN BE EXPLORED IN THE PRACTICE OF PUPPETRY.

ONE HISTORICAL SOURCE OF PUPPETRY IS THE HAN DYNASTY, ESTABLISHED IN 202 BCE.

PUPPETS IN CHINA ARE THOUGHT TO DERIVE FROM STATUETTES THAT WERE BURIED WITH EMPERORS.

DRAGON KILN

THIS, INSTEAD OF BURYING THEM WITH FORMERLY ALIVE HUMANS AS "COMPANIONS IN DEATH."

33

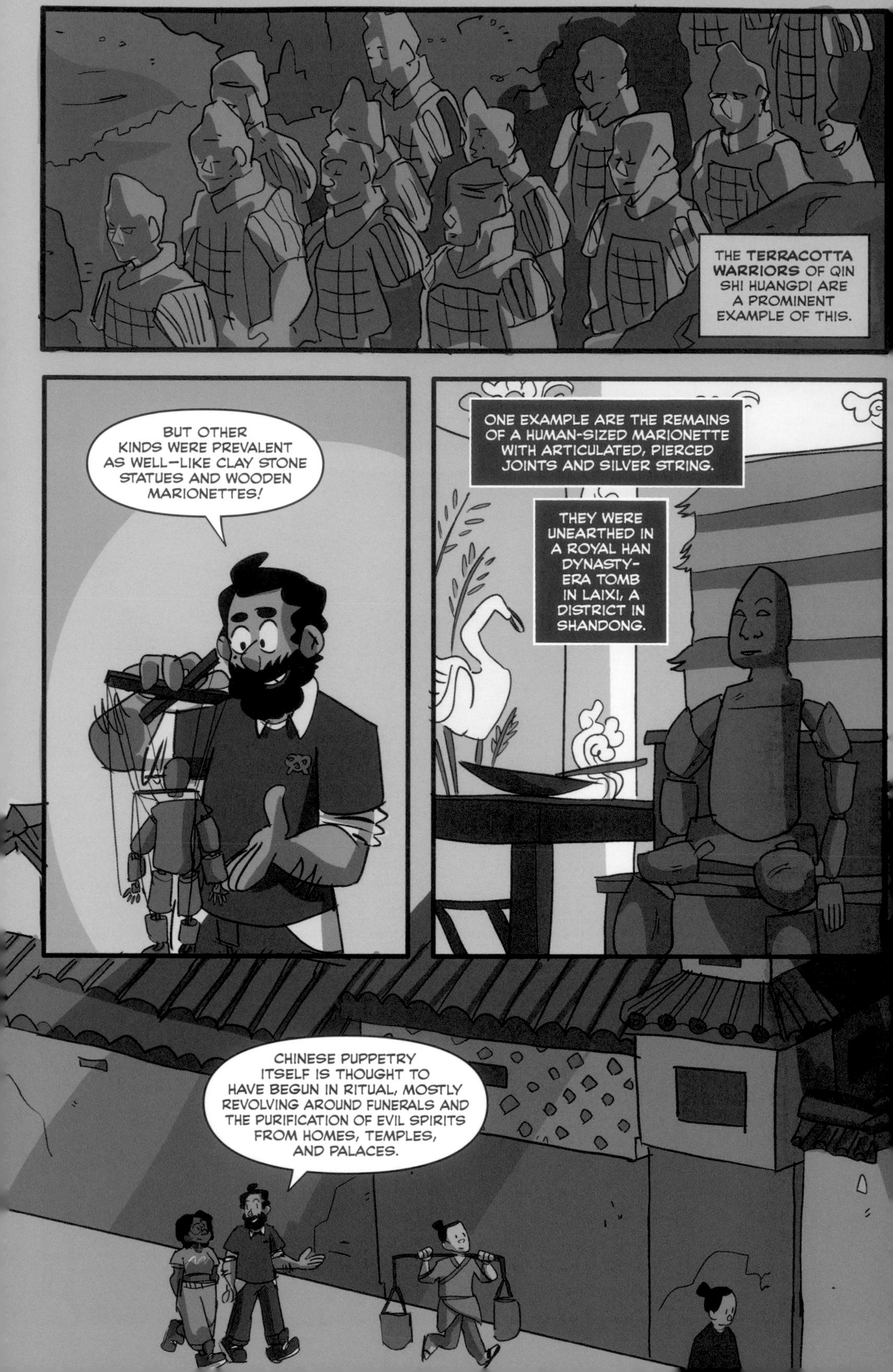
THE TERRACOTTA WARRIORS OF QIN SHI HUANGDI ARE A PROMINENT EXAMPLE OF THIS.
BUT OTHER KINDS WERE PREVALENT AS WELL—LIKE CLAY STONE STATUES AND WOODEN MARIONETTES!
ONE EXAMPLE ARE THE REMAINS OF A HUMAN-SIZED MARIONETTE WITH ARTICULATED, PIERCED JOINTS AND SILVER STRING.
THEY WERE UNEARTHED IN A ROYAL HAN DYNASTY-ERA TOMB IN LAIXI, A DISTRICT IN SHANDONG.
CHINESE PUPPETRY ITSELF IS THOUGHT TO HAVE BEGUN IN RITUAL, MOSTLY REVOLVING AROUND FUNERALS AND THE PURIFICATION OF EVIL SPIRITS FROM HOMES, TEMPLES, AND PALACES.

HERE WE ARE IN A NEW HOUSE, WHERE AN EXORCISM PLAY CALLED *ZHAO XUANTAN TAMES THE TIGER* IS BEING PUT ON.

BASED IN LEGEND, ZHAO XUANTAN, ONE OF NINE SUNS THAT WAS BROUGHT TO EARTH, BECAME KNOWN AS A POWERFUL DEITY.

SO POWERFUL THAT PERFORMING HIS RITUAL PLAY WOULD CAUSE A NESTING DEMON TO FLEE A NEW HOUSE IN TERROR, LEAVING IT IN PEACE.

FOR LARGER AND MORE IMPORTANT STRUCTURES, LIKE THIS TEMPLE, THE SAME IDEA OF PUPPETRY APPLIED BUT ON A MUCH LARGER SCALE.

EVEN MORE POWERFUL PLAYS WERE NEEDED TO BANISH MORE POWERFUL EVIL SPIRITS.

THESE RITUAL PLAYS DATED BACK TO THE ZHOU DYNASTY (1046–256 BCE).

THEY COMBINED ELEMENTS FROM CONFUCIANISM, TAOISM, AND MYANMAR BUDDHISM, WHICH WERE BECOMING PROMINENT DURING THE HAN DYNASTY.

THOUGH IT'S DIFFICULT TO SAY FOR SURE, PUPPETRY IS THOUGHT TO HAVE BEEN USED FOR RITUALS AND RITUAL CELEBRATIONS.

LIKE MARRIAGES, FOR EXAMPLE.

OR KUILEI WEI SANGJIA YUE*, WHICH WERE FUNERAL RITUALS THAT INCLUDED A FORM OF ENTERTAINMENT.

*TRANSLATION: FUNERAL PUPPETRY

FROM THE MOMENT THESE PUPPETS ENTERED THE STAGE, A SPECIAL RELATIONSHIP OF TRUST BEGAN BETWEEN THE PERFORMERS AND THE AUDIENCE. THESE WERE RITUALS, BUT THEY WERE ALSO PERFORMANCES, THE LATTER OF WHICH BECAME PREVALENT DURING THE HAN DYNASTY.

WARRIOR TALES, RECOUNTING ACTUAL EVENTS CELEBRATING HAN DYNASTY MILITARY VICTORIES, BECAME POPULAR AND HAD POLITICAL SIGNIFICANCE, AS OPPOSED TO JUST BEING RITUAL.

IF YOU ARE SO CAPABLE, THEN WHY ARE YOU ONE OF MY SUBJECTS, HAN XIN?

YOUR POSITION IS MANDATED BY THE HEAVENS, MY SOVEREIGN. IT IS NOT SOMETHING HUMANS CAN CHANGE.

THEN WHY WERE YOU TAKEN CAPTIVE BY ME?

YOUR MAJESTY CANNOT COMMAND THE TROOPS BUT IS GOOD AT COMMANDING THE COMMANDERS.

THE GREAT GENERAL HAN XIN IS AN EXAMPLE OF SUCH A PLAY. AS ONE OF THE "THREE HEROES OF THE EARLY HAN DYNASTY," HAN XIN'S STORY WAS RETOLD IN EPIC PROPORTIONS.

WARRIOR TALES SHOW THAT THE HAN DYNASTY CAN BE THOUGHT OF AS THE EARLIEST PRACTITIONERS OF HISTORICAL REENACTMENT.

TODAY'S REENACTMENTS—MOSTLY CENTERED AROUND BATTLES—ARE EDUTAINMENT EVENTS. BUT THEY SERVE A SIMILAR PURPOSE AS ANCIENT WARRIOR TALES.

SINCE THE HAN DYNASTY'S UNIFICATION WAS SEEN AS A MASSIVE ACCOMPLISHMENT, THEY NEEDED TO BECOME IMPORTANT PARTS OF CULTURAL MEMORY.

HAVE MERCY, HAN XIN!

WARRIOR TALES REINFORCED THAT IMPORTANCE THROUGH PERFORMANCE.

THEY MAY HAVE ALSO SERVED AS STATE PROPAGANDA IN THE CASE OF THE HAN DYNASTY, TO LEGITIMIZE THE EMPEROR'S RIGHTFUL RULE.

HISTORICAL REENACTMENT LETS PEOPLE SAFELY INHABIT OTHER ROLES, BECOMING HEROES AND VILLAINS.

THEY CAN SIMULATE INVOLVEMENT IN MONUMENTAL EVENTS WITHOUT PARTICIPATING IN THEM DIRECTLY.

KIND OF LIKE WHEN I PLAYED TEENAGE MUTANT NINJA TURTLES AS A KID. BUT, *UH*, SAFER.

HAN XIN, HAVE MERCY!

EVENTUALLY, PUPPETRY WAS BEING USED FOR BOTH RITUAL AND ENTERTAINMENT PURPOSES—OFTEN IN COMBINATION!

THE **BAIXI**, OR A HUNDRED ENTERTAINMENTS, WERE A BIG PART OF THAT.

BY 229 BCE, HAN EMPEROR WUDI HAD ESTABLISHED WHAT WAS KNOWN AS BAIXI, OR "A HUNDRED ENTERTAINMENTS."

THIS WAS A FESTIVAL THAT FEATURED PUPPETEERS, JUGGLERS, MAGICIANS, ACROBATS, DANCING, AND MARTIAL ARTS DEMONSTRATIONS.

BUT **THE HORN-BUTTING GAME** STANDS OUT AMONG THE REST, AS A COMBINATION OF MARTIAL ARTS AND PERFORMANCE!

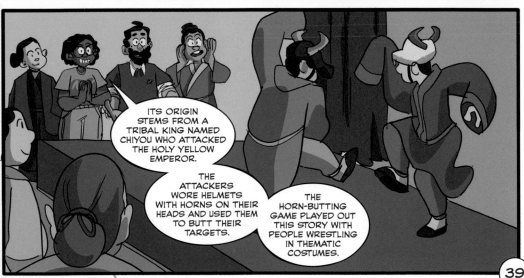

ITS ORIGIN STEMS FROM A TRIBAL KING NAMED CHIYOU WHO ATTACKED THE HOLY YELLOW EMPEROR.

THE ATTACKERS WORE HELMETS WITH HORNS ON THEIR HEADS AND USED THEM TO BUTT THEIR TARGETS.

THE HORN-BUTTING GAME PLAYED OUT THIS STORY WITH PEOPLE WRESTLING IN THEMATIC COSTUMES.

THESE PERFORMANCES EVENTUALLY PICKED UP ELABORATE TALES, SUCH AS HUANG OF THE EASTERN SEA, TELLING THE STORY OF A MAGICIAN WHO, DESPITE HIS HEROISM, FAILS AT DEFEATING A LEGENDARY WHITE TIGER.

PERFORMERS USED PROPS AND INTERACTED WITH THE AUDIENCE. IT'S EVEN POSSIBLE THAT THE OUTCOME OF THE STORY COULD HAVE CHANGED DEPENDING ON HOW THE AUDIENCE REACTED.

HE'S TOO OLD!

DON'T DOUBT! HE'S STILL GOT THE SWORD!

TO ME, THE HORN-BUTTING GAME RESEMBLES PROFESSIONAL WRESTLING.

THOUGH THE ACTION IS CHOREOGRAPHED, THE AUDIENCE IS MEANT TO TREAT IT AS SPONTANEOUS. THE FIGHTING ACTORS WERE NOT JUST PANTOMIMING A STORY.

THEY WERE TRYING TO SIMULATE BATTLE IN A REALISTIC MANNER WITHOUT ACTUALLY HURTING THEIR OPPONENT. WHICH IS WHY THE GAME ENDED UP HAVING A VERSION USED FOR MARTIAL ARTS TRAINING EXERCISES.

STORYTELLING IS A FUNDAMENTAL PART OF HUMAN BEHAVIOR.

WHEN YOU READ OR HEAR A STORY, YOU FORM A RELATIONSHIP WITH IT. YOU BECOME INVESTED AS IT PULLS YOU ALONG.

AND WHEN YOU FEEL YOU ARE ABLE TO PARTICIPATE IN A STORY, THE ACTIONS AND THEMES ARE MORE POWERFUL.

BECOMING AN ACTUAL PARTICIPANT IN A STORY IS A FUNDAMENTAL PART OF TTRPGS.

AND THAT CONCEPT IS ANYTHING BUT MODERN.

SO IF YOU CAN'T TELL, WE'RE LAYING OUT THE FOUNDATION FOR WHAT MAKES THESE GAMES WHAT THEY ARE.

WHICH MEANS TALKING ABOUT THE ORIGINS OF ANOTHER BIG PART OF TTRPGS...

THE TABLETOP.

SO BEFORE WE HEAD BACK TO THE GAME ROOM, LET'S EXPLORE THE ORIGINS OF TACTICAL TABLETS, STRATEGIZING SURFACES, BEGUILING BILLETS!!

THE GAME BOARD!

TO INDIA!

PATALIPUTRA, INDIA
SIXTH CENTURY
THE GUPTA EMPIRE

NICE DIGS!

CHATURANGA IS ONE OF THE OLDEST STRATEGY GAMES IN THE WORLD. IT'S ALSO A PRECURSOR TO CHESS.

YOU CAN SEE THE SIMILARITIES IN CHATURANGA'S LAYOUT.

BUT THERE ARE SOME DIFFERENCES—LIKE THE NAMES!

AND SOME OF THE PIECES MOVED DIFFERENTLY AS WELL.

ALTHOUGH THE RAJA, ASHVA, BHATA, AND RATHA MOVED MUCH LIKE THEIR MODERN COUNTERPARTS, THE MANTRI—UNLIKE THE QUEEN—WAS ONLY ABLE TO MOVE DIAGONALLY.

THE GAJA COULD ALSO MOVE DIAGONALLY LIKE A BISHOP, BUT NOT AS FAR, AND IT COULD ALSO JUMP.

CHATURANGA ALSO HAD A FOUR-PLAYER VARIATION CALLED CHATURAJI, WHICH INVOLVED DICE AND PIECES THAT INCLUDED NAVAL SHIPS.

AS WAS THE CASE WITH BOARD GAMES IN MANY CULTURES, CHATURANGA WAS PLAYED BY THE NOBILITY.

THERE WAS AN EXPRESS AIM FOR THIS: TO MAKE PEOPLE WITH STATUS INTO BETTER LEADERS AND STRATEGISTS.

THEY TRAINED FOR LEADERSHIP BY MODELING THEIR ABILITY TO UNDERSTAND THE BATTLEFIELD.

A GOOD LEADER WAS A GOOD GENERAL. AND A GOOD GENERAL WON WARS.

IN CHATURANGA'S CASE IN PARTICULAR, LIKE OTHER WAR-STRATEGY GAMES WE'LL ENCOUNTER, IT WASN'T AVAILABLE FOR THE NON-ELITE TO PLAY.

CHATURANGA WASN'T JUST A GAME. IT WAS A WAY TO CULTIVATE POWER.

43

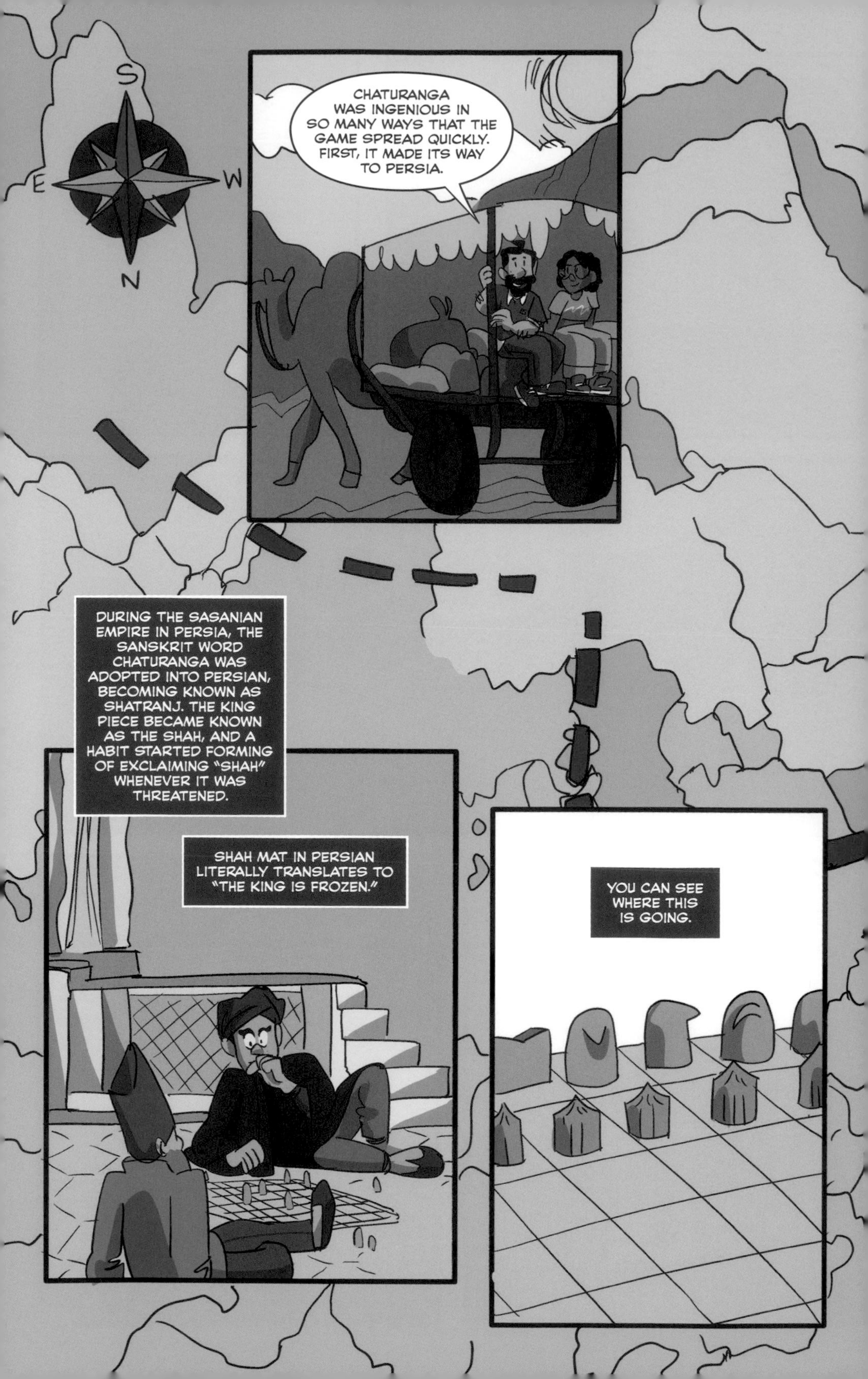

S
E
W
N
CHATURANGA WAS INGENIOUS IN SO MANY WAYS THAT THE GAME SPREAD QUICKLY. FIRST, IT MADE ITS WAY TO PERSIA.
DURING THE SASANIAN EMPIRE IN PERSIA, THE SANSKRIT WORD CHATURANGA WAS ADOPTED INTO PERSIAN, BECOMING KNOWN AS SHATRANJ. THE KING PIECE BECAME KNOWN AS THE SHAH, AND A HABIT STARTED FORMING OF EXCLAIMING "SHAH" WHENEVER IT WAS THREATENED.
SHAH MAT IN PERSIAN LITERALLY TRANSLATES TO "THE KING IS FROZEN."
YOU CAN SEE WHERE THIS IS GOING.

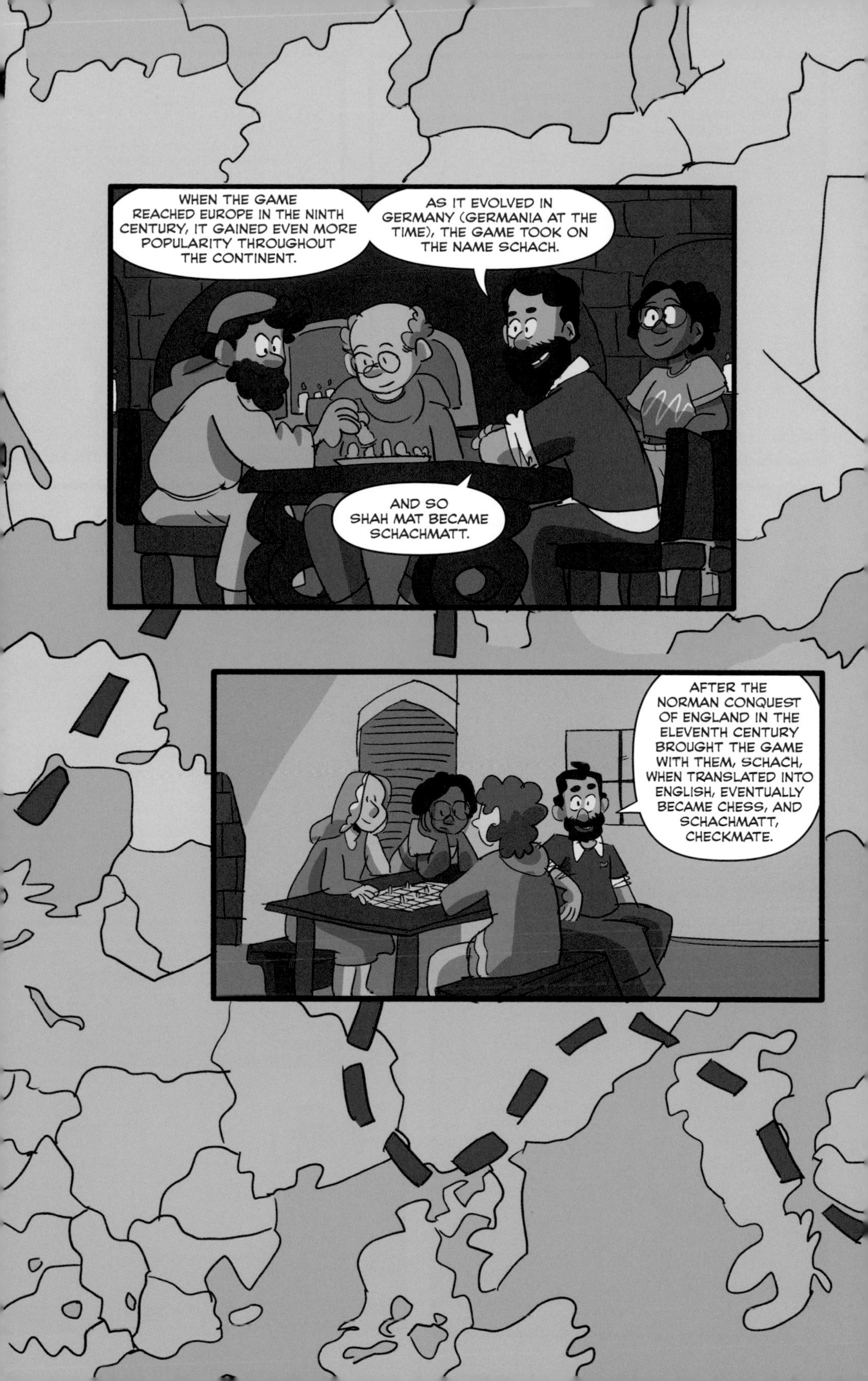
WHEN THE GAME REACHED EUROPE IN THE NINTH CENTURY, IT GAINED EVEN MORE POPULARITY THROUGHOUT THE CONTINENT.
AS IT EVOLVED IN GERMANY (GERMANIA AT THE TIME), THE GAME TOOK ON THE NAME SCHACH.
AND SO SHAH MAT BECAME SCHACHMATT.
AFTER THE NORMAN CONQUEST OF ENGLAND IN THE ELEVENTH CENTURY BROUGHT THE GAME WITH THEM, SCHACH, WHEN TRANSLATED INTO ENGLISH, EVENTUALLY BECAME CHESS, AND SCHACHMATT, CHECKMATE.

WE'RE OVERSIMPLIFYING THINGS A BIT, OF COURSE. SHATRANJ SPREAD THROUGH A VARIETY OF NATIONS IN SOUTHERN EUROPE AND ASIA AS WELL, AND TOOK ON VARIOUS FORMS.

MOST COUNTRIES HAVE A VERSION OF CHESS IN THEIR HISTORY, DERIVED FROM SHATRANJ OR NOT.

THOUGH WHAT WAS ORIGINALLY CHATURANGA ENDED UP EXERTING THE MOST GLOBAL INFLUENCE, OTHER SIMILAR BOARD GAMES HAVE BEEN UNEARTHED FROM AROUND THE ANCIENT WORLD AND STILL REMAIN POPULAR TODAY.

GAMES LIKE CHATURANGA WERE CREATED TO MODEL BATTLE, SPECIFICALLY USING STRATEGY TO OUTTHINK YOUR OPPONENT.

BUT EVEN THOUGH CHATURANGA IS INTELLECTUALLY RIGOROUS, IT'S HARD TO LOOK AT IT AS SIMULATING ACTUAL WARFARE.

WHILE IT TAKES A LOT OF THOUGHT TO MASTER A KNIGHT ON THE BOARD, IT WON'T PREPARE YOU TO COMMAND ACTUAL CAVALRY.

AND IT'S KINDA HARD TO GIVE CHARACTER TRAITS TO THESE SIMPLE, ONE-FUNCTION TOKENS.

BUT CHATURANGA AND CHESS DID LEAD TO GAMES THAT CAME CLOSER TO SIMULATING MILITARY CAMPAIGNS, WHICH BECAME A BIG PART OF MODERN TTRPGS.

SOME FIND COMPLEX MILITARY SIMULATION GAMES DISCONCERTING, SINCE THEY CAN BE SAID TO GLORIFY ACTUAL VIOLENCE AND DOMINATION.

BUT AS YOU'LL SOON SEE, WITHOUT THEM, WE WOULDN'T HAVE ARRIVED AT THE CREATION OF DUNGEONS & DRAGONS.

NEW THINGS COME FROM SHARING IDEAS. CREATIVITY DOESN'T THRIVE IN A VACUUM.

I KNOW THAT NOW. BUT WHEN I WAS YOUNGER, THAT IDEA DIDN'T MAKE SENSE TO ME.

IF SOME-THING WAS SUPPOSED TO LOOK, WORK, AND FEEL A CERTAIN WAY, HOW COULD IT BREAK FROM THAT MOLD?

BUT MY IDEAS OF CREATIVITY AND INNOVATION WERE CHALLENGED WHEN MY DAD TOLD ME HE USED TO PLAY DUNGEONS & DRAGONS WHEN HE WAS YOUNGER.

WE PLAYED DUNGEONS & DRAGONS FOR THREE HOURS!

DUNGEONS & DRAGONS?! THAT'S SO NERDY...

DID YOU SAY D&D? I USED TO PLAY THAT!

REALLY?!

I COULDN'T IMAGINE MY DAD PLAYING SOMETHING THAT LOOKED TO ME LIKE IT WAS JUST OLD WHITE WIZARDS AND THEIR WHITE COMPANIONS FIGHTING TROLLS.

SO YOU PLAYED...A WHITE WIZARD?

WELL... MORE LIKE A WHITE ELF. BUT THAT'S WHAT THE MODELS WERE.

HM.

ANYWAY.

BUT IT WASN'T ALL LIKE THAT!

DEITIES & DEMIGODS

I HAD A D&D BOOK CALLED DEITIES & DEMIGODS. AND THERE WERE THESE EGYPTIAN GODS IN THERE.

AND WHILE THEY LOOKED WHITE, I IMAGINED THEM TO LOOK LIKE US, TO ACTUALLY LOOK BLACK.

HUH... COOL!

WERE YOU INTERESTED IN PLAYING D&D OR SOMETHING?

NOPE.

HAH, OKAY. WELL, YOU LET ME KNOW.

I DIDN'T THINK TOO MUCH OF IT THEN BECAUSE I STILL NEVER PLAYED ANY KIND OF TABLETOP ROLEPLAYING GAME UNTIL I WAS AN ADULT.

BUT THE IDEA HAD BEEN PLANTED IN MY HEAD THAT THINKING OUTSIDE OF THE BOX WAS A POSSIBILITY.

AND WHEN YOU THINK OUTSIDE OF THE BOX, THINGS EVOLVE AND SO HAVE TTRPGS.

THAT'S A PART OF WHAT MAKES THEM SO INTERESTING TO ME.

WHAT ARE YOU LOOKING FOR?

HERE IT IS!

Patolli

HERE WHAT IS?

A GAME WITH AN INTERESTING DIE.

Patolli

OH, I'VE SEEN THIS BEFORE...

IT'S NOT A POLYHEDRAL DIE, BUT NONETHELESS.

YES! THIS WAS USED TO PLAY THE GAME PATOLLI!

THAT'S RIGHT! FROM MESOAMERICA.

KLAK!

SPECIFICALLY, AROUND 750 BCE...

PATOLLI IS A STRATEGY GAME, BUT UNLIKE CHATURANGA AND CHESS, IT UTILIZES A BOARD AND DICE.

AND EVEN MORE NOTABLY, IT REVOLVES AROUND GAMBLING.

PLAYERS WOULD BET EVERYTHING FROM BLANKETS AND JEWELRY TO THEIR OWN HOMES OR EVEN THEIR FAMILIES.

HARSH.

KLAK!

GAMES LIKE PATOLLI COULD HAVE REAL-LIFE CONSEQUENCES.

PLEASE! I SHOULDN'T HAVE BET MY HOME. WHERE WILL MY FAMILY SLEEP?

TELL IT TO THE GODS, PAL.

ALL DEPENDENT ON THESE LITTLE DICE.

GAMES AND DICE HAVE A LONG AND HAPPY HISTORY. BUT THEY DIDN'T ALWAYS GO HAND IN HAND.

ALL RIGHT, WHO'S NEXT?

WHAT'S YOUR OFFERING?

IN MANY SOCIETIES OVER TIME, DICE HAVE BEEN USED TO REFLECT THE WILL OF DIVINE BEINGS.

WHEN YOU ROLLED ONE WAY, YOU COULD EXPECT POWERFUL FORCES TO WEIGH IN ACCORDINGLY.

YOU WILL HAVE A SON THIS YEAR.

IN PATOLLI, WHATEVER YOU ROLLED WAS THOUGHT TO REFLECT THE WILL OF THE GODS, PARTICULARLY THE GOD OF GAMBLING, MACUILXOCHITL. WHEN PLAYING THE GAME, PARTS OF THE BOARD WOULD BE DESIGNATED FOR AN OFFERING.

WHEN YOU WON A ROUND, IT WAS LIKE WINNING A GIFT FROM MACUILXOCHITL HIMSELF! A REWARD FOR A LIFE WELL LIVED. WHILE THE LOSER, PRESUMABLY NOT FAVORED BY THE GOD OF GAMBLING, HAD TO PAY THE PRICE.

DICE GAMES EXIST ACROSS THE ANCIENT WORLD, AND SOME, LIKE PATOLLI, WERE IMBUED WITH SPIRITUAL MEANING.

IN OTHER CULTURES, DICE WERE USED STRICTLY FOR MYSTICAL PURPOSES. NO ONE KNOWS WHEN DIVINATION GAVE WAY TO GAMING, BUT THE TWO ARE INEXTRICABLY LINKED.

SO WHY ARE WE TALKING ABOUT THE MYSTIC ROOTS OF DICE?

WELL, EVEN THOUGH WE DON'T REALLY ASSOCIATE DICE WITH DIVINE FORCES WHILE PLAYING GAMES ANYMORE, THEIR MYSTICAL ROOTS HAVEN'T FADED.

IN THE 1980S, ACADEMIC GARY ALAN FINE CARRIED OUT STUDIES ON TTRPG PLAYERS.

HE FOUND THAT THEY ARE INCREDIBLY SUPERSTITIOUS ABOUT DICE, TO THE POINT WHERE THEY BELIEVE CERTAIN SETS ROLL BETTER THAN OTHERS.

SHAKE SHAKE

EXCLUDING WEIGHTED DICE, OF COURSE.

WHICH DICE ARE YOUR LUCKIEST?

ALL OUR DICE ARE LUCKY, KID.

BOTH PLAYERS AND GMS BLAME THEIR OWN ROLLING ABILITIES WHEN THEY AREN'T ACHIEVING THE RESULTS THEY WANT, AS IF THE ROLLING OF DICE ISN'T LEFT UP TO PROBABILITY BUT SOME KIND OF OUTSIDE FORCE.

GAMES LIKE PATOLLI, WHICH WERE THOUGHT TO DEAL DIRECTLY WITH DIVINE FORCES, HAVE LEFT THEIR MARK ON MODERN TTRPGS.

BECAUSE PLAYERS AND GMS BARGAIN WITH FATEFUL FORCES, WHETHER THEY BELIEVE IN THEM OR NOT.

I SAY THIS NOT ONLY AS AN OBSERVER BUT A PARTICIPANT.

DENVER, COLORADO, USA
SAM'S FRIEND'S BACKYARD
1996

ATTACK! ATTACK THE FIEND!

YOU SURE ABOUT THAT?

I'M PRETTY SURE I'M FOURTEEN HERE.

WHAT ELSE AM I SUPPOSED TO DO?

YOU'VE BEEN ROLLING LIKE CRAP.

SO HAVE YOU.

WELL, ADVENTURERS, IT SEEMS AS IF YOU'VE HIT A BOUT OF BAD LUCK.

MIGHT I SUGGEST YOU... RETREAT?

IT MUST BE THESE DICE.

THESE DICE SUCK!

YEAH!

NEW DICE!

REALLY? YOU GUYS, DICE ARE JUST DICE. YOU CAN'T FIX BAD LUCK.

SO SAYS THE DM THAT'S BEEN ROLLING TWENTIES ALL DAY. I'M GETTING ANOTHER SET.

CHECK THESE OUT.

LEMME SEE THOSE...

HMM... YEAH...I LIKE HOW THESE FEEL. MUCH BETTER.

THEY FEEL THE EXACT SAME!!

NOW I'M READY TO ATTACK.

DON'T SAY I DIDN'T WARN YOU...

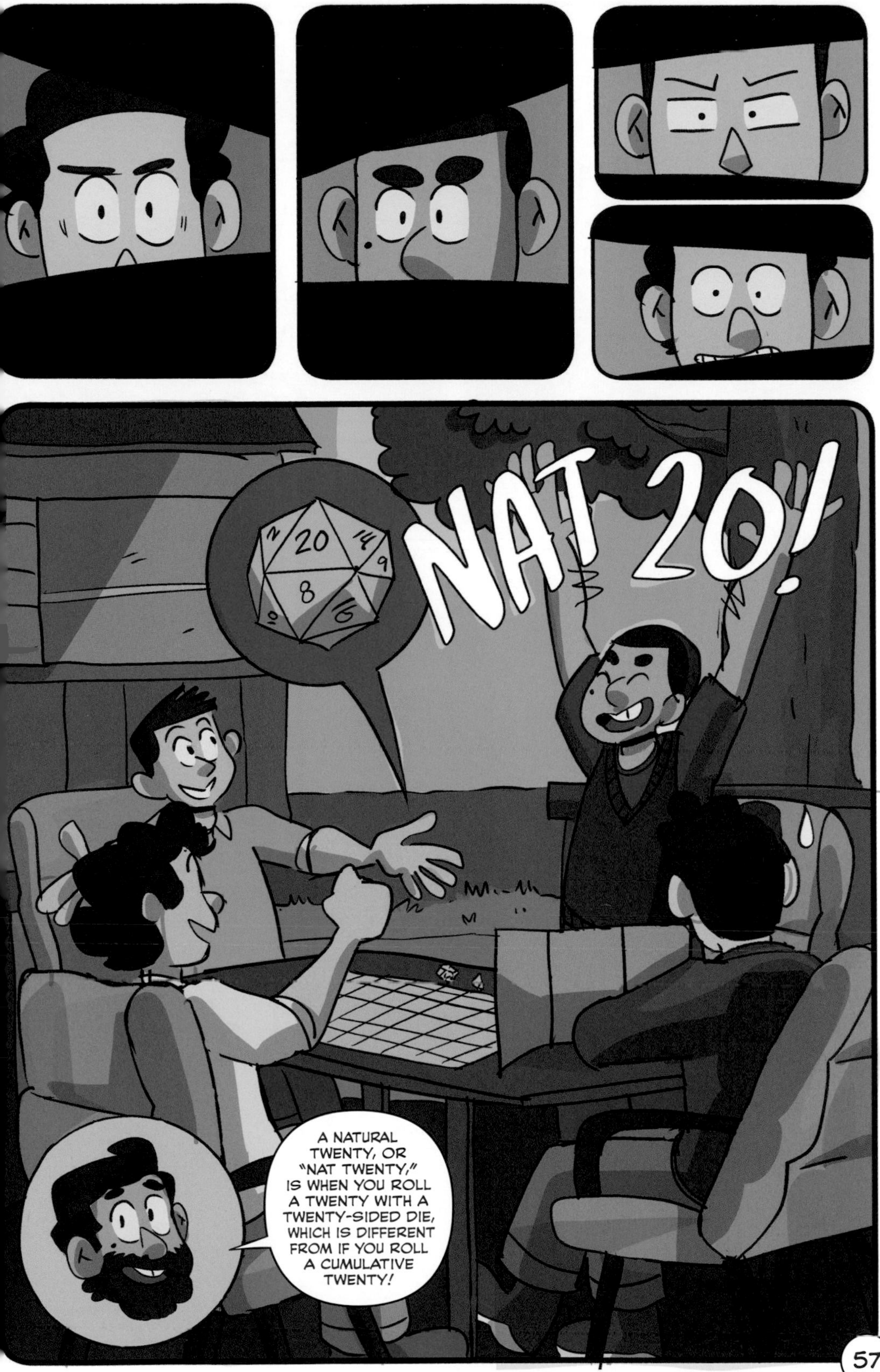
NAT 20!
A NATURAL TWENTY, OR "NAT TWENTY," IS WHEN YOU ROLL A TWENTY WITH A TWENTY-SIDED DIE, WHICH IS DIFFERENT FROM IF YOU ROLL A CUMULATIVE TWENTY!

WHATEVER. DOESN'T MEAN ANYTHING.

THE OGRE OF HILLSDOWN ATTACKS, AND...

WHAT?!

SLAM!

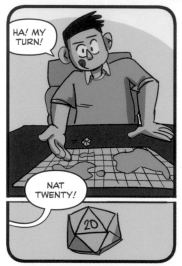

HA! MY TURN!

NAT TWENTY!

YES! NINETEEN!

EIGHTEEN DAMAGE!

WELL, THAT'S THE END OF MY OGRE...

YOU GUYS ARE OUT OF YOUR MIND.

SO WHAT DO YOU **REALLY** THINK? WAS THAT NEW SET OF DICE ACTUALLY LUCKIER THAN THE OTHER?

CAN'T SAY EITHER WAY...ALL I KNOW IS THAT OUR LUCK IMPROVED RIGHT AFTER WE SWITCHED OUT THOSE DICE.

I ALSO THINK WHAT YOU EXPERIENCED TIES INTO RULE-BENDING.

IT'S NOT A ONE-TO-ONE COMPARISON, BUT WHEN YOU BEND RULES IN A TTRPG, YOU DO SO BECAUSE YOU BELIEVE THE ADVENTURE ITSELF IS MORE IMPORTANT THAN THE RULES.

ALTERING RULES IS COMMON PRACTICE IN TTRPGS. EVEN PEOPLE WHO LIKE TO PLAY BY THE BOOK WILL LET SOMETHING SLIP BY IF IT IMPROVES THE GAMING EXPERIENCE. CHECK OUT THESE FOLKS, FOR EXAMPLE.

OKAY, THE ROCK OGRE ATTACKS YOU...

I DODGE THE ATTACK!

DID IT... DID IT HIT ME?

UH...

NO. IT ROLLED A THIRTEEN! CLOSE ONE.

THIS ISN'T TRUE IN GAMES LIKE CHESS, WHERE THE GAME MECHANICS DON'T ALLOW FOR LENIENCY.

CLOSE ONE? WHAT DID I NEED TO ROLL TO DODGE?

I GAVE YOU SOME SLACK. YOU WOULD HAVE NEEDED SEVENTEEN TO SUCCEED!

A SEVENTEEN?! I WOULD HAVE RUN AWAY IF I'D KNOWN THAT! MY CHARACTER WILL DIE IF I TAKE THIS KIND OF DAMAGE!

FINE. YOU CAN REROLL.

DOES THIS MEAN THAT TTRPGS DON'T HAVE SOLID RULE SYSTEMS? NOT AT ALL. BUT WHEN YOU ARE ROLEPLAYING, OUTCOMES CAN FEEL PERSONAL. THE QUESTION FOR PLAYERS OFTEN COMES DOWN TO:

WOULD I HAVE DONE THAT IN REAL LIFE?

TTRPGS ALLOW PLAYERS TO IMMERSE THEMSELVES IN AN IMAGINED REALITY WHERE THEY FEEL LIKE THEIR CHARACTERS (AND CHOICES) ARE EXTENSIONS OF THEMSELVES.

KIND OF LIKE WITH THE HORN-BUTTING GAME. IF THE STORY NEEDS TO BEND TO SATISFY THE AUDIENCE IN REAL TIME, THEN IT WILL.

TTRPGS AREN'T COMPETITIVE IN THE WAY CHECKERS, CHESS, OR MANY OTHER TABLETOP GAMES ARE, BUT THEY DO REQUIRE INVESTING EMOTIONAL CURRENCY, AND GAME PLAY CAN BLEED INTO EVERYDAY LIFE. THEY CAN BE TESTING GROUNDS FOR GAINING NEW SKILLS, SIMULATING NEW IDENTITIES, OR EVEN BUILDING AND EXECUTING PERSONAL GOALS.

SO WE WERE GETTING ATTACKED BY THIS HORDE OF GOBLINS BECAUSE JARGUS STOLE THEIR LOOT—FREAKING SOCIOPATH.

BUT SINCE MY CHARACTER LOATHES BLOODSHED, I CRUMBLED A CAVE WALL SO WE COULD RUN AWAY. AND NO ONE GOT HURT!

YOU KNOW, I ALWAYS TRY TO PLAY ANTIHEROES, BUT... IT WAS KINDA NICE TO JUST DO SOMETHING GOOD.

THEN MAYBE THE GAME'S TRYING TO TELL YOU SOMETHING. REMEMBER HOW YOU MENTIONED LOOKING INTO BECOMING AN EMT?

HUH. YEAH... MAYBE I SHOULD DO THAT...

IT IS OFTEN REPORTED THAT TTRPG PLAYERS HAVE EXPERIENCES IN GAME THAT ALTER THEIR OUTLOOKS ON LIFE.

THESE GAMES AREN'T JUST FUN BUT USEFUL.

61

FOR CENTURIES, PEOPLE HAVE DEVELOPED MORE INTERACTIVE WAYS TO SIMULATE WARFARE. AND IN PART, TTRPGS AROSE DIRECTLY FROM THAT.

THE IMPORTANCE OF WARGAMING IN PARTICULAR FEELS A LITTLE UNCOMFORTABLE TO THINK ABOUT.

JUST THE IDEA OF WAR BEING A GAME IS A DISCUSSION IN ITSELF.

BUT WARGAMES ARE A LOT MORE THAN MEETS THE EYE, PARTICULARLY WHEN IT COMES TO CONNECTING THEM TO REAL-WORLD VIOLENCE.

WARGAMES (OR *KRIEGSSPIEL* IN GERMAN) IS A SEPARATE CATEGORY FROM OTHER BATTLE-FOCUSED GAMES.

KRIEGSPIEL

CHESS CAN *KIND OF* BE CONSIDERED A GAME THAT DEALS WITH WARFARE.

KRIEGSPIEL

BUT THIS CATEGORY IS UNIQUE UNTO ITSELF.

PIEL

Part Three

FROM BATTLEFIELD TO SANDTABLE

WARGAMES CAME TO USE DICE, STATISTICS, AND A TABLETOP BOARD SETUP THAT WOULD CONTINUE INTO THE TWENTIETH CENTURY...

THEY ARE ENCODED INTO THE DNA OF DUNGEONS & DRAGONS AND OTHER FANTASY RPGS LIKE IT.

SO LET'S HAVE A LOOK AT WHERE THESE GAMES GOT THEIR START.

HELMSTADT, GERMANY
1780

THIS GENTLEMAN IS **JOHANN CHRISTIAN LUDWIG HELLWIG**, A GERMAN ENTOMOLOGIST, MATHEMATICS PROFESSOR, AND GAME DESIGNER.

WHILE TEACHING MATH AT THE MILITARY ACADEMY OF BRAUNSCHWEIG IN 1780, HE CREATED A BOARD GAME TO HELP WITH THE INSTRUCTION OF MILITARY SCIENCE.

WE LOOK TO MINIMIZE THE FOG AND FRICTION OF WAR.

HELLWIG'S GOAL WAS TO BUILD UPON CHESS AND CHESS VARIATIONS TO CREATE A GAME THAT MORE ACCURATELY DEPICTED WAR SCENARIOS AND THAT COULD BE PLAYED WITH TWO OR MORE PLAYERS FOR LEARNING PURPOSES.

WHERE CHESS IS A GAME THAT MODELS THE BATTLEFIELD IN AN ABSTRACT SENSE, WARGAMES AIM FOR *ACCURACY*.

THE RESULT WAS AN EARLY VERSION OF KRIEGSPIEL.

IT HAD CUSTOMIZABLE TERRAIN THAT INFLUENCED THE WAYS UNITS COULD MOVE AND ATTACK.

THERE WERE NO DICE, BUT ITS LANDSCAPE INNOVATIONS AND TACTICAL PIECE MOVEMENTS WOULD LEAD TO WARGAMING'S EVOLUTION.

ABOUT THIRTY YEARS LATER IN POTSDAM, GERMANY, THIS PRUSSIAN ARMY OFFICER GEORGE LEOPOLD VON REISSWITZ WAS INSPIRED BY HELLWIG'S CREATION.

THE MAN HE'S SPEAKING WITH IS KING FRIEDRICH WILHELM III, WHO RULED OVER PRUSSIA DURING THE NAPOLEONIC WARS.

MY, MY, OFFICER REISSWITZ...THIS IS DELIGHTFUL!

A MOCK WAR IN A CABINET. QUITE THE FEAT.

I'M GLAD YOU THINK SO, YOUR MAJESTY.

YES...WITH EUROPE AT WAR, WE MUST MAINTAIN OUR EDGE.

WE WILL GIVE A KRIEGSPIEL CABINET TO EVERY GENERAL IN PRUSSIA!

AS LONG AS WE CAN GET PAST THE PROBLEM OF PRODUCTION...

IN GEORGE LEOPOLD'S VERSION OF KRIEGSPIEL, TERRAIN WAS TAKEN TO A WHOLE NEW LEVEL. EACH TILE WAS ELABORATELY DETAILED AND COULD BE LAID OUT IN CUSTOM ORDER.

THE TILES FEATURED RIVERS, MOUNTAINS, BRIDGES, FORESTS, AND OTHER ELEMENTS COMMON TO ANY BATTLEFIELD.

THOUGH THIS ROYAL VERSION OF THE GAME WAS PREFABRICATED, SOME GAMES WOULD BE PLAYED ON MOLDABLE SAND, WHICH IS WHY SOME WARGAMERS REFER TO THE TABLETOP AS "THE SANDBOX."

THESE PORCELAIN PIECES SYMBOLIZED ACTUAL MILITARY UNITS AND COULD BE PUT INTO A NEAR-ENDLESS VARIETY OF FORMATIONS.

INFANTRY, HORSEMEN, CUIRASSIERS, HEAVY ARTILLERY, AND HOWITZERS WERE JUST SOME OF THE UNITS YOU COULD PLAY WITH.

ADVANCES IN CARTOGRAPHY PROVIDED MORE ACCURATE WAYS TO TRACK DISTANCE ON MAPS.

THERE WERE ALSO NAVAL PIECES, A SEXTON, AND SIX-SIDED DICE TO DECIDE BASIC COMBAT PROBABILITIES. THOUGH NOT USED MUCH AT FIRST, BY 1824 THEY'D BECOME AN INTEGRAL PART OF PLAY.

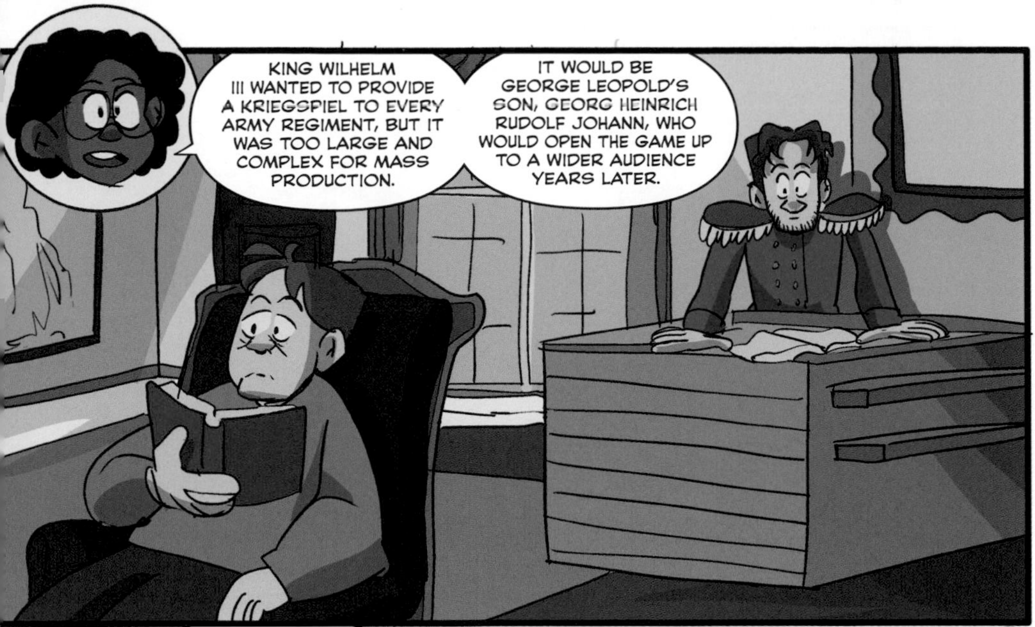
KING WILHELM III WANTED TO PROVIDE A KRIEGSPIEL TO EVERY ARMY REGIMENT, BUT IT WAS TOO LARGE AND COMPLEX FOR MASS PRODUCTION.
IT WOULD BE GEORGE LEOPOLD'S SON, GEORG HEINRICH RUDOLF JOHANN, WHO WOULD OPEN THE GAME UP TO A WIDER AUDIENCE YEARS LATER.

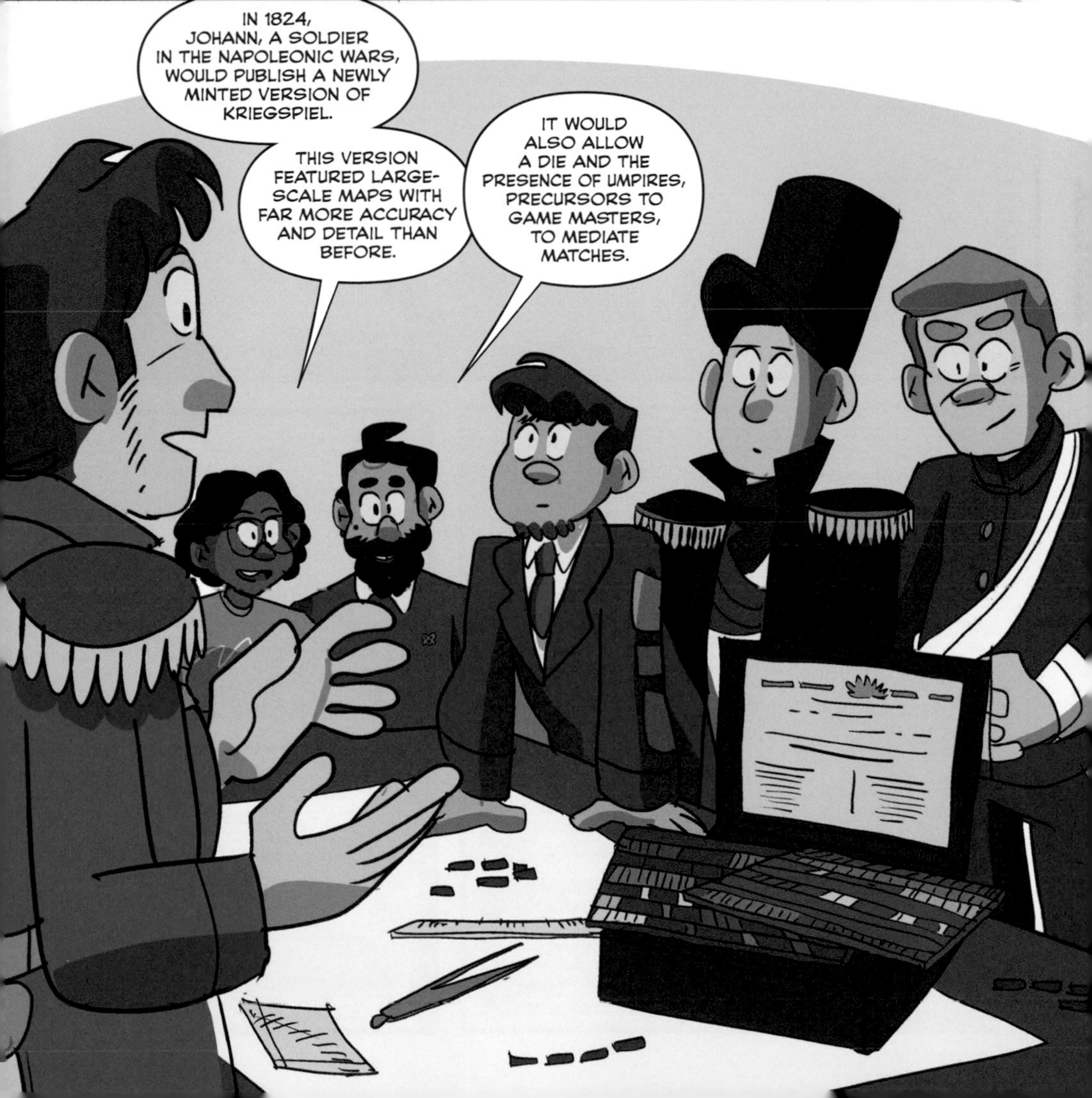
IN 1824, JOHANN, A SOLDIER IN THE NAPOLEONIC WARS, WOULD PUBLISH A NEWLY MINTED VERSION OF KRIEGSPIEL.
THIS VERSION FEATURED LARGE-SCALE MAPS WITH FAR MORE ACCURACY AND DETAIL THAN BEFORE.
IT WOULD ALSO ALLOW A DIE AND THE PRESENCE OF UMPIRES, PRECURSORS TO GAME MASTERS, TO MEDIATE MATCHES.

THE UMPIRE PLAYED A UNIQUE ROLE, NOT ONLY DECIDING THE STARTING ARMY SIZE AND COMPOSITION FOR EACH PLAYER, BUT RECEIVING THEIR DECISIONS AND INTERPRETING THEM PROPERLY. THIS MEANS THAT EACH SIDE HAD TO ACCEPT THE OUTCOME OF THEIR DECISIONS THROUGH A THIRD PARTY. FOR COMBAT, THE POWER STATISTICS OF EACH OPPOSING ARMY INTERACTED WITH DICE ROLLS TO DECIDE THE OUTCOME.

WHEN THE NEWLY REDESIGNED KRIEGSPIEL EMERGED IN 1824, KING WILHELM III REQUESTED IT BE DISTRIBUTED WIDELY TO THE MILITARY. FROM THERE, IT HEADED TOWARD MASS PRODUCTION. JOHANN WORKED WITH PAINTERS, CARPENTERS, A TIN FOUNDRY, AND THE ROYAL LITHOGRAPHIC INSTITUTE TO CREATE A VIABLE COMMERCIAL PRODUCT THAT FIT INTO A TEN-BY-SIX-INCH BOX.

BY THE LATE 1800S, THIS VERSION OF KRIEGSPIEL WAS BEING TRANSLATED INTO VARIOUS LANGUAGES, LIKE ENGLISH. IT SPREAD TO BRITAIN IN THE 1870S, AND EVENTUALLY TO THE UNITED STATES, EVOLVING WHEREVER IT LANDED.

EVENTUALLY, IT FOUND ITS WAY TO **CHARLES ADIEL LEWIS TOTTEN,** AN AMERICAN MILITARY OFFICER, PROFESSOR, AND WRITER.

A GAME OF WAR AND STRATEGY. WHAT A LARK.

ONE, PLEASE!

INSPIRED BY KRIEGSPIEL, TOTTEN CAME UP WITH A GAME OF HIS OWN: **STRATEGOS**, THE AMERICAN GAMES OF WAR, IN 1880.

REMARKABLE! WE CAN USE THIS IN THE FIELD.

BASIC RULES OF STRATEGOS—REVAMPED BY DAVID A. WESLEY IN 1970 AND RENAMED STRATEGOS N—ARE A VARIATION ON KRIEGSPIEL, WITH RULES AND PIECES BASED ON REALISTIC MILITARY STRATEGY.

MORE ADVANCED RULES INVOLVED MAPS AND A REFEREE/UMPIRE TO MODERATE THE GAME.

KRIEGSPIEL STARTED WITH BASIC TILES OR BLOCKS TO REPRESENT TROOPS.

BUT AS TIME WENT ON, TOY SOLDIERS WOULD BE BROUGHT INTO THE MIX.

ROME   MAYA   EGYPT

THE ORIGIN OF MILITARY FIGURINES IS ANCIENT. THEY HAVE APPEARED IN MOST CULTURES AROUND THE WORLD.

THEY WERE PUT INTO WIDESPREAD PRODUCTION IN THE EIGHTEENTH CENTURY, PRODUCED IN GERMANY FROM TIN. THEY BECAME EVEN MORE POPULAR IN BRITAIN IN 1893, AFTER THE TOY COMPANY WILLIAM BRITAIN CREATED HOLLOW CASTING. BRITAIN WAS THE HUB FOR TOY SOLDIER PRODUCTION, UNTIL WORLD WAR I PIVOTED PRODUCTION TOWARD WARTIME NEEDS.

FIGURINES OR MINIATURES ARE USED TO REPRESENT *PLAYER CHARACTERS*, *NONPLAYER CHARACTERS*, AND ADVERSARIES IN GAMES.

I LOVE PAINTING FIGURINES. IT'S ONE OF THE THINGS I LIKE MOST ABOUT TTRPGS...

AND IN A LOT OF SITUATIONS, I PREFER IT TO ACTUAL GAME PLAY.

REMINDS ME OF A TIME...

OOHOO, A BAG FROM THE COMIC SHOP!

GOT ANY TREATS FOR ME? *HEH HEH?*

HEY! YOU GOT A MINI FOR YOUR D&D GAME.

OH YEAH, *HEH.* I WAS ACTUALLY GOING TO ASK IF YOU WANTED TO PAINT IT FOR ME. I'M NOT THAT CREATIVE...

AW, I'D LOVE TO!

BUT LET ME DO SOME RESEARCH FIRST.

SAM S.

STEENZ

What paint should I get?

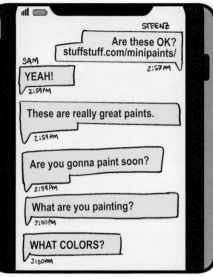

STEENZ

Are these OK? stuffstuff.com/minipaints/

2:57PM

SAM

YEAH!

2:59PM

These are really great paints.

2:59PM

Are you gonna paint soon?

2:59PM

What are you painting?

3:00PM

WHAT COLORS?

3:00PM

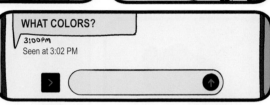

WHAT COLORS?

3:00PM

Seen at 3:02 PM

WHEN I WAS PAINTING THESE FIGURES, I LOST TIME.

GETTING THE RIGHT COLORS, FIGURING OUT OF THE SIZE OF BRUSHES, SMALL DETAILS—IT'S ALL EXCITING!

I FELT LIKE I WAS BRINGING HIS CHARACTER TO LIFE!

ALL DONE!

WHOA! THIS LOOKS *AMAZING.*

YEAH, IT'S PRETTY NICE, IF I DO SAY SO MYSELF...GOT ANYMORE?

WELL, YOU CAN ALWAYS PAINT YOUR OWN, YANNO, IF YOU JOIN THE CAMPAIGN.

MMM...

PASS.

BEING INTERESTED IN PARTS OF THE TABLETOP ROLEPLAYING PROCESS AND COMMUNITY IS JUST AS VALID AS BEING A TTRPG SUPERFAN.

CORRECT!

WHEN IT COMES TO GAMES, I PREFER MORE TACTILE EXPERIENCES. FIGURINES ALLOW FOR THAT.

AND THEY'RE CUSTOMIZABLE!

FIGURINES, TOY SOLDIERS IN PARTICULAR, BECAME A FACET OF WARGAMES WITH THE INVENTION OF **LITTLE WARS**.

THE GAME WAS CREATED IN 1913 AND BY AN INTERESTING CHARACTER: THE FAMOUS SCIENCE FICTION WRITER H. G. WELLS.

WELLS HAD TENDENCIES TOWARD ANTI-SEMITISM, RACISM, AND SEXISM THAT BELIE HIS LEGACY TO THIS DAY. BUT LOOKING AT HIS REASONS FOR CREATING LITTLE WARS IS WORTHWHILE.

A NOTED ANTIWAR ADVOCATE, WELLS, WHO HAD PLAYED KRIEGSPIEL, WAS DISILLUSIONED WITH THE GAME'S LACK OF IMAGINATION, OVERLY BAROQUE RULES, AND RELIANCE ON UMPIRES.

THIS IS A MESS!

WHEN PLAYING LITTLE WARS, PLAYERS WOULD SOMETIMES PAINT THEIR FIGURINES.

THEY ALSO UNDERSTOOD THAT THOSE FIGURINES WOULD GET BANGED UP. WELLS WAS REALLY BIG ON THE IDEA OF NOT BEING GENTLE ON YOUR TOYS.

THE RULES INVOLVED SOME DICE ROLLING, BUT MOSTLY THEY WERE GOVERNED BY SET MOVEMENT AND UNIT-STRENGTH PARAMETERS.

HONESTLY, THE MOST INNOVATIVE THING ABOUT LITTLE WARS WAS ITS VISUAL DESIGN.

FULL-SCALE TERRAINS WERE CREATED, CALLING FOR CRAFTSMANSHIP AND CREATIVITY. PEOPLE STILL DO IT TO THIS DAY IN SCI-FI/FANTASY GAMES LIKE WARHAMMER.

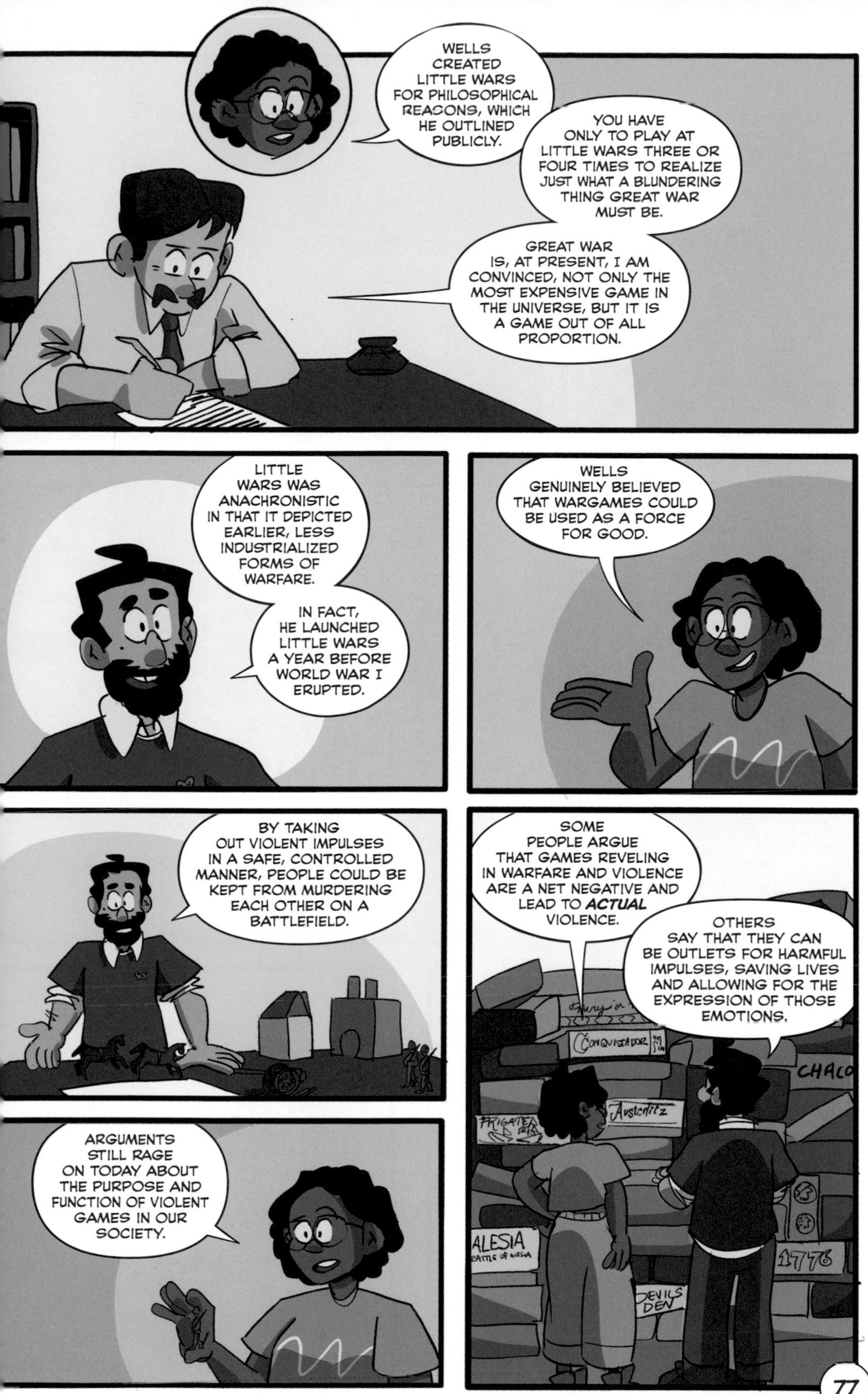
WELLS CREATED LITTLE WARS FOR PHILOSOPHICAL REASONS, WHICH HE OUTLINED PUBLICLY.
YOU HAVE ONLY TO PLAY AT LITTLE WARS THREE OR FOUR TIMES TO REALIZE JUST WHAT A BLUNDERING THING GREAT WAR MUST BE.
GREAT WAR IS, AT PRESENT, I AM CONVINCED, NOT ONLY THE MOST EXPENSIVE GAME IN THE UNIVERSE, BUT IT IS A GAME OUT OF ALL PROPORTION.
LITTLE WARS WAS ANACHRONISTIC IN THAT IT DEPICTED EARLIER, LESS INDUSTRIALIZED FORMS OF WARFARE.
IN FACT, HE LAUNCHED LITTLE WARS A YEAR BEFORE WORLD WAR I ERUPTED.
WELLS GENUINELY BELIEVED THAT WARGAMES COULD BE USED AS A FORCE FOR GOOD.
BY TAKING OUT VIOLENT IMPULSES IN A SAFE, CONTROLLED MANNER, PEOPLE COULD BE KEPT FROM MURDERING EACH OTHER ON A BATTLEFIELD.
ARGUMENTS STILL RAGE ON TODAY ABOUT THE PURPOSE AND FUNCTION OF VIOLENT GAMES IN OUR SOCIETY.
SOME PEOPLE ARGUE THAT GAMES REVELING IN WARFARE AND VIOLENCE ARE A NET NEGATIVE AND LEAD TO ***ACTUAL*** VIOLENCE.
OTHERS SAY THAT THEY CAN BE OUTLETS FOR HARMFUL IMPULSES, SAVING LIVES AND ALLOWING FOR THE EXPRESSION OF THOSE EMOTIONS.
CONQUISTADOR
Austerlitz
ALESIA
BATTLE OF ALESIA
1776
DEVILS DEN

REGARDLESS, IT'S WORTH NOTING THAT WELLS'S GAME LED TO THE INCREASED DEVELOPMENT OF WARGAMES FOR GENERAL AUDIENCES. IN OTHER WORDS, FOR FUN!

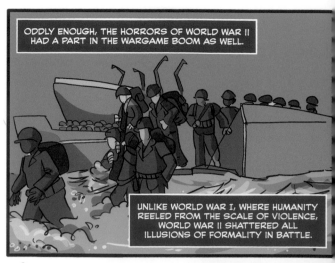

ODDLY ENOUGH, THE HORRORS OF WORLD WAR II HAD A PART IN THE WARGAME BOOM AS WELL.

UNLIKE WORLD WAR I, WHERE HUMANITY REELED FROM THE SCALE OF VIOLENCE, WORLD WAR II SHATTERED ALL ILLUSIONS OF FORMALITY IN BATTLE.

THIS WAS DUE TO THE TECHNOLOGY EMPLOYED DURING WORLD WAR II, WHICH WAS DEADLIER AND MORE UNTESTED THAN ANYTHING ELSE ENCOUNTERED THROUGHOUT HISTORY.

THE MOMENT THE ATOM BOMB WAS DROPPED, *CONVENTIONAL* WARFARE CAME TO AN END.

THE AGE OF WAR AS A GENTLEMAN'S SPORT, WITH FESTOONED UNIFORMS AND BLOCKED BATTLEFIELD FORMATIONS, WAS OFFICIALLY OVER.

AND THE AGE OF MODERN WARFARE BEGAN...

WHEN I WAS TWELVE YEARS OLD, ONE OF MY FRIENDS AT THE TIME INTRODUCED ME TO A GAME I WOULD BECOME OBSESSED WITH.

SO OBSESSED I WANTED TO PLAY EVERY DAY IF I COULD.

RIVALING MY LOVE OF DUNGEONS & DRAGONS WAS THE STRATEGY WARGAME AXIS & ALLIES. ALLOWING YOU TO CHOOSE ONE OF THE TWO SIDES DURING WWII, THE GAME TOOK ITS INFLUENCE FROM WARGAMES OF THE PAST, CONCENTRATING ON RESOURCE MANAGEMENT AND GEOGRAPHICAL DOMINATION.

THE FRIEND I OFTEN PLAYED WITH, LIKE ME, WAS JEWISH, SO WE OFTEN TRIED TO PAWN OFF THE AXIS.

I BETTER NOT GET STUCK WITH THE NAZIS AGAIN.

THE GAME WOULD LAST LONG INTO THE NIGHT DURING SLEEPOVERS.

AND EVENTUALLY, I BECAME INTERESTED IN THE HISTORY ACCOMPANYING IT.

I KNEW A TINY BIT ABOUT WORLD WAR II RELATING TO ITS ATROCITIES, BUT LITTLE MORE.

THERE WAS SOMEONE WHO DID KNOW, HOWEVER...

MY GRANDPA.

MY GRANDPA WAS A STOIC MAN. AND ONE I DIDN'T KNOW VERY WELL.

THIS WAS DUE MOSTLY, AS I UNDERSTOOD IT, TO HIS EXPERIENCES IN THE WAR.

YOU ALREADY FINISHED, GRANDPA?

YOUR GRANDPA EATS QUICK, HONEY. IT'S FROM HIS TRAINING IN THE WAR.

SOMETIMES HE WOULD OPEN UP ABOUT LESS SERIOUS TOPICS...

ONE TIME, I DECIDED TO GO TO SWITZERLAND, TO GO SKIING. WENT COMPLETELY AWOL.

NO ONE KNEW WHERE I WAS, BUT I DIDN'T CARE! I HAD TO LET OFF SOME STEAM.

BUT HE WAS CAGIER ABOUT HEAVIER STUFF.

BUT, GRANDPA, HOW DID YOU GET THAT RINGING IN YOUR EAR?

OH... WELL, THAT WAS, *EH*...

I WAS A DEMOLITION MAN, YOU'D CALL IT. I HAD TO BLOW UP BRIDGES.

ONE EXPLOSION WAS SO LOUD THAT I BLEW MY EARDRUM OUT. HAD THAT RINGING EVER SINCE. I PARACHUTED INTO NORMANDY. LOTS DEAD ON THE WAY DOWN...

WERE YOU SCARED?

TERRIFIED.

WE...WE LIBERATED A CAMP. A CONCENTRATION CAMP.

THE MAYOR, HE PRETENDED TO NOT KNOW ANYTHING ABOUT WHAT WAS GOING ON INSIDE.

SO I SAID, OH, YEAH? WELL, YOU AND *YOUR* PEOPLE ARE GOING TO BURY THE BODIES.

THE DETAILS I LEARNED FROM MY GRANDPA WEREN'T HEARTWARMING BY ANY STRETCH. BUT THEY DID OPEN MY MIND AS TO WHAT IT MIGHT HAVE BEEN LIKE TO BE IN A WAR, AS OPPOSED TO PLAYING A SIMULATED ONE, WHICH IS WHAT I'D DONE UP TO THAT POINT.

FROM THEN ON, AXIS & ALLIES TOOK ON A NEW MEANING TO ME. IN THE FUTURE, I'D THINK HOW STRANGE IT WAS THAT THE GAME TOOK SUCH A COMPLEX PART OF HISTORY AND MADE IT A COMPETITIVE PASTIME.

LOOKING BACK, I SEE HOW GAMES CAN LEAD TO UNEXPECTED DISCOVERIES ABOUT OURSELVES AND THE REAL WORLD.

AND I WONDER IF THAT'S ONE OF THE REASONS WE ENJOY THEM.

YOUR GRANDPA SEEMED INTENSE.

HE WAS!

ALTHOUGH MOSTLY I REMEMBER HIM AS SOMEONE WHO FELL ASLEEP A LOT WHILE WATCHING TV.

Part Four
ASSUME YOUR ROLE

GAMES CONNECT US TO THE REAL WORLD IN A LOT OF WAYS...

TTRPGS EVEN MORE SO BECAUSE OF HOW THEY TRY TO GET CLOSER TO A REAL-SEEMING EXPERIENCE.

"SEEMING" IS THE KEY WORD. YOU WOULDN'T WANT A GAME TO LEAVE THE REALM OF THE IMAGINATION AND ENTER REALITY. LIKE IN ANCIENT ROME...

ROME
85 CE

WHOA.

THIS IS A **NAUMACHIA!** A GIGANTIC STAGED NAVAL BATTLE IN ANCIENT ROME.

NAUMACHIA CELEBRATED THE SPECTACLE OF COMPETITIVE VIOLENCE. IN MANY WAYS, THEY WERE EXTENSIONS OF GLADIATORIAL COMBAT WE ASSOCIATE WITH THE HISTORIC COLOSSEUM, BUT ON A MASSIVE SCALE.

AND YEAH, DESPITE ITS... DEPRAVITY, NAUMACHIAE WERE CONSIDERED **GAMES**— JUST AS MUCH SPECTACLE AS THEY WERE COMPETITIONS.

THIS PARTICULAR NAUMACHIA WAS STAGED BY EMPEROR DOMITIAN TO CELEBRATE HIS RECENT SUCCESSION.

HE'D STAGE ANOTHER AFTER HIS VICTORY IN DACIA IN 86 CE, DIGGING A GIANT POOL NEAR TIBER TO HOLD IT.

USUALLY THEY DID NAUMACHIA AFTER A VICTORY IN BATTLE, TO CELEBRATE. WHICH IS WHY THEY WERE OFTEN REENACTMENTS OF THE BATTLES THEY JUST WON.

BUT UNLIKE WITH THE WARRIOR TALES OF ANCIENT CHINA, THESE GAMES ACTUALLY HAD LIFE-AND-DEATH STAKES.

WITHIN THE CONFINES OF AN AMPHITHEATER FILLED WITH METRIC TONS OF WATER, THOUSANDS OF COMBATANTS AND ROWERS, ALL PRISONERS OF WAR, WOULD PARTICIPATE IN A FIGHT TO THE ACTUAL DEATH.

THE MORE WHO DIED, THE BETTER, ACCORDING TO ROMAN AUTHORITIES. TYPICALLY, NEAR NONE WERE LEFT ALIVE.

ROMANS WOULD FORCE THE PRISONERS OF WAR TO CARRY THE FLAG OF THEIR FORMER KINGDOM INTO BATTLE.

THEY HAD TO RELIVE THEIR BRUTAL DEFEAT, THIS TIME BEFORE THE CHEERS AND JEERS OF THEIR CONQUERORS.

I THINK MOST OF US WOULD AGREE THAT THESE SPECTACLES WERE BRUTAL AND CRUEL.

THEY STAKED MASSIVE AMOUNTS OF LIFE AND RESOURCES ON THE CELEBRATION OF BLOODY SUBJUGATION, BY ATTEMPTING TO RELIVE THEM IN REAL TIME.

BUT NAUMACHIAE DO PROVIDE INSIGHT INTO WHY TTRPGS RESONATE SO MUCH WITH US TODAY.

PARDON.

87

HUMANS HAVE ALWAYS BEEN DRAWN TO SIMULATING THE REAL WORLD IN GAMES.

THIS IS DIFFERENT FROM TEAM SPORTS.

WITH TEAM SPORTS, THE GOAL ISN'T TO RECREATE HISTORICAL EVENTS IN ORDER TO BETTER UNDERSTAND OR CELEBRATE THEIR SIGNIFICANCE.

THE GOAL IS TO COMPETE ATHLETICALLY FOR VICTORY.

EVENTS LIKE NAUMACHIAE RELY ON FOLKS WANTING TO SIMULATE REAL IMPULSES SO VIVIDLY THAT THEY CROSS TOO FAR OVER INTO REALITY.

TTRPGS UNDERSTAND THIS DYNAMIC WELL. THIS IS WHY THEY STRIVE TO CREATE SITUATIONS THAT SIMULATE REALITY FROM A PSYCHOLOGICAL STANDPOINT, WHILE MAINTAINING SAFE BOUNDARIES.

SAFE BOUNDARIES MEANING THEY DON'T INVOLVE ACTUAL MURDER.

LET'S TAKE A LOOK AT THIS DUNGEONEERING PARTY AS AN EXAMPLE.

I'D LIKE TO TRY AND STEAL HIS COIN PURSE.

ROLL FOR SLEIGHT OF HAND TO SEE IF YOU SUCCEED...

WHAT TTRPGS OFFER PEOPLE IS A PLATFORM TO CREATE SPACES WHERE IMAGINATION CAN BE SHARED.

AS YOU ATTEMPT TO CUT THE CYBORG'S COIN PURSE, YOU FAIL TO NOTICE THE ROBOTIC FERRET HIDING IN HIS POCKET!

A STORYTELLER SETS UP THE FRAMEWORK FOR THAT SHARED SPACE, AND THE PLAYERS CONTRIBUTE TO THE STORY, CHANGING IT.

HEY!

HISS!!

THE CREATURE MAKES A ROBOTIC SCREECH! YOU'VE BEEN CAUGHT.

89

UGH, WHY MUST YOU ALWAYS STEAL?

A BETTER QUESTION:

HOW DO WE GET OUT OF THIS MESS?

WELL, I WON'T STAND FOR THIS!

WHETHER YOU STAND FOR IT OR NOT, YOU'RE BOTH ABOUT TO GET ATTACKED. ROLL FOR INITIATIVE.

WITH NAUMACHIAE, THE ARENA IS LIFE-AND-DEATH, WHILE IN TTRPGS, EMOTIONS ARE AT STAKE. THIS IS WHY COMMUNITY BECOMES SUCH AN IMPORTANT PART OF PLAY.

AND WHAT BETTER TO SHOWCASE A COMMUNITY THAN... THE THEATER!

FLORENCE, ITALY
SIXTEENTH CENTURY

LET'S GET TO THE FRONT!

THEATER! *WOOO!!*

COMMEDIA DELL'ARTE TRANSLATES ROUGHLY TO "COMEDY OF THE PROFESSION," BUT IS KNOWN AS ITALIAN COMEDY.

IN IT, ACTORS WOULD IMPROVISE THEIR PERFORMANCES BASED ON SKETCHES OR SCENARIOS THEY MADE UP.

WHAT ARE WE GOING TO DO WITH THIS FOOL, *EH?*

THROW HIM OUT!

YEAH! DO AWAY WITH HIM!

ABBIAMO UN DUELLO?

MAMMA MIA!

COMMEDIA DELL'ARTE AROSE FROM **FABULA ATELLANA**, A FORM OF ITALIAN DRAMATIC FARCE THAT ORIGINATED IN THE CAMPANIA REGION OF SOUTHERN ITALY. IT CAN BE COMPARED TO THE HORN-BUTTING GAME BUT SILLIER.

PROPS, LAZZI (IMPROVISED STOCK ROUTINES), AND AUDIENCE PARTICIPATION BECAME THIS FORM OF THEATER'S FOUNDATIONS, WHICH RELIED ON THE AUDIENCE TO FINISH OUT AN ACT.

THERE ISN'T A TABLETOP INVOLVED IN COMMEDIA DELL'ARTE. BUT ROLEPLAYING DEFINITELY IS.

YOU COULD SAY THAT THE AUDIENCE ARE THE PLAYERS AND THE ACTORS ARE GAME MASTERS!

AQUA?

COMMEDIA DELL'ARTE IS RELIANT ON COMMUNITY PARTICIPATION. AND AS WE MENTIONED EARLIER, THAT'S A HUGE PART OF WHAT GOES INTO PLAYING TTRPGS.

THOUGH THERE ARE SOME EXCEPTIONS AMONG GAMES BASED ON THEIR DESIGN MECHANICS, ACTUAL ROLEPLAYING REQUIRES INTERACTING WITH OTHERS.

I'M INTERESTED IN SEEING WHERE THE TERM "ROLEPLAYING" ACTUALLY CAME FROM.

VIENNA
1920S

LET'S FIND OUT!

A MEETING OF TWO: EYE TO EYE, FACE TO FACE.

AND WHEN YOU ARE NEAR, I WILL TEAR YOUR EYES OUT AND PLACE THEM INSTEAD OF MINE, AND YOU WILL TEAR MY EYES OUT AND WILL PLACE THEM INSTEAD OF YOURS, THEN I WILL LOOK AT YOU WITH YOUR EYES AND YOU WILL LOOK AT ME WITH MINE.

THE MAN SPEAKING IS *JACOB LEVY MORENO.*

BORN IN 1889 IN BUCHAREST, ROMANIA, HE'S KNOWN AS THE CREATOR OF DRAMA THERAPY IN THE WEST, BEGINNING WITH WHAT HE CALLED "PSYCHODRAMA."

AND HE WAS THE FIRST PERSON TO COIN THE TERM:

ROLEPLAYING.

JACOB MORENO WAS WORKING IN THE TIME OF SIGMUND FREUD, FOUNDER OF WESTERN PSYCHOANALYSIS. WHILE ADMIRING MUCH OF FREUD'S WORK, HE WAS SIMULTANEOUSLY CRITICAL OF HIM.

PSYCHO-THERAPY
• THE UNCONSCIOUS
○ DREAMS

SCIENCE
PHILOSOPHY

I ALWAYS FIND THE SAME PRINCIPLES CONFIRMED: THE ELEMENTS FORMED INTO THE DREAM ARE DRAWN FROM THE ENTIRE MASS OF THE DREAM-THOUGHTS.

AND IN ITS RELATION TO THE DREAM-THOUGHTS, EACH ONE OF THE ELEMENTS SEEMS TO BE DETERMINED MANY TIMES OVER.

WELL, DR. FREUD, I START WHERE YOU LEAVE OFF.

YOU MEET PEOPLE IN THE ARTIFICIAL SETTING OF YOUR OFFICE. I MEET THEM ON THE STREET AND IN THEIR HOMES, IN THEIR NATURAL SURROUNDINGS.

YOU ANALYZE THEIR DREAMS. I GIVE THEM THE COURAGE TO DREAM AGAIN.

JACOB MORENO, LIKE **CARL JUNG**, BELIEVED IN THERAPY REACHING BROADER BEYOND FREUD'S NOTION OF THE UNCANNY.

EXPLORATION OF THE PSYCHE IS ACHIEVED THROUGH COMMUNITY.

AS AN EDUCATOR AND PSYCHOANALYST, JACOB WANTED TO SHINE A POSITIVE LIGHT ON THERAPY THROUGH ACTIVE EXPRESSION.

SO HE INVENTED PSYCHODRAMA.

THE AUDIENCE SEES ITSELF—THAT IS, ONE OF ITS COLLECTIVE SYNDROMES—PORTRAYED ON THE STAGE.

PSYCHODRAMA USES SELF-PRESENTATION AND DRAMATIC PERFORMANCE—WHAT MORENO REFERRED TO AS ROLEPLAYING—IN ORDER TO CONDUCT IMPROVISED THEATER. HIS IDEAS FOR THERAPY REVOLVED AROUND ADOPTING ROLES, SOME OF WHICH WERE UNCOMFORTABLE.

HE USED PROPS. HE ENCOURAGED PLAY. HE DELIGHTED IN THE IMAGINATION GAMES THAT CHILDREN PARTICIPATED IN AND THOUGHT THEY COULD BE USED TO HELP PEOPLE HEAL.

PSYCHODRAMA IS A WAY TO CHANGE THE WORLD IN THE HERE AND NOW USING THE FUNDAMENTAL RULES OF IMAGINATION WITHOUT FALLING INTO THE ABYSS OF ILLUSION, HALLUCINATION, OR DELUSION.

THE HUMAN BRAIN IS THE VEHICLE OF THE IMAGINATION!

WHILE NOT MENTIONED OFTEN ENOUGH, MORENO WOULD CONTRIBUTE GREATLY TO A VARIETY OF MODERN THERAPY METHODS, MOST NOTABLY GESTALT THERAPY, IN WHICH THERAPISTS USE PROPS, GUIDED IMAGERY, AND ROLEPLAYING FOR TREATMENT.

GROUP THERAPY PROBABLY WASN'T SOMETHING YOU EXPECTED TO BE A MAJOR CONTRIBUTOR TO MODERN TTRPGS, BUT THE MORE YOU THINK ABOUT IT, THE MORE SENSE IT MAKES.

TTRPGS CAN LEAD TO A LOT OF POSITIVE CHANGES IN A PERSON'S LIFE.

PLAYERS EXPLORE THEIR CHARACTER'S PERSONALITY, DISCOVERING NEW THINGS.

THE CHARACTER BECOMES AN EXTENSION OF THE UNCONSCIOUS SELF.

AS THE COLLECTIVE UNCONSCIOUS CONTENTS ARE CONCERNED, WE ARE DEALING WITH ARCHAIC OR, I WOULD SAY, PRIMORDIAL TYPES—THAT IS, WITH UNIVERSAL IMAGES THAT HAVE EXISTED IN SOME CULTURES SINCE THE REMOTEST TIMES.

CARL JUNG, THE FOUNDER OF WESTERN ANALYTICAL PSYCHOLOGY, WROTE ABOUT THE MYRIAD ROLES HE BELIEVED HUMANS HAVE STORED IN THEIR COLLECTIVE UNCONSCIOUS—ROLES THAT WE TAP INTO OVER THE COURSE OF OUR LIVES.

THESE ROLES, WHICH HE CALLED ARCHETYPES, TEND TO REPEAT IN HERO STORIES THROUGHOUT VARIOUS GLOBAL HISTORIES.

THE EXPLORER

THE MAGICIAN.

THE HERO.

THE RULER.

JUNG'S ARCHETYPES HAVE BEEN CRITIQUED BY SOME, PARTICULARLY WHEN IT COMES TO DECONSTRUCTING GENDER. BUT THEY STILL OFFER MANY INSIGHTS.

JUNG ENCOURAGED HIS PATIENTS TO UNDERSTAND WHICH OF HIS ARCHETYPES THEY RELIED UPON. YOU WERE ASKED TO INHABIT, OR ROLEPLAY, UNFAMILIAR PARTS OF YOURSELF.

IN TTRPGS, PLAYERS TAKE ON ROLES THAT APPEAL TO THEM FOR A VARIETY OF REASONS. SOME PEOPLE MIGHT CHOOSE A CHARACTER THAT REFLECTS THEIR OWN VALUES AND IDEAS, WHILE OTHERS MAY GO OUTSIDE OF THEIR COMFORT ZONE, CHOOSING TO EXPAND THEIR HORIZONS.

IN SHORT, WHEN PLAYERS TAKE ON CHARACTERS, THEY ACCESS, OR DISCOVER, DIFFERENT PARTS OF THEMSELVES!

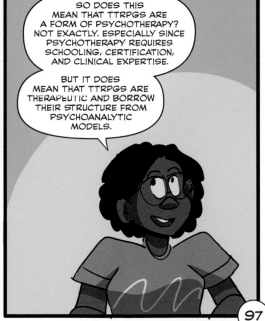

SO DOES THIS MEAN THAT TTRPGS ARE A FORM OF PSYCHOTHERAPY? NOT EXACTLY. ESPECIALLY SINCE PSYCHOTHERAPY REQUIRES SCHOOLING, CERTIFICATION, AND CLINICAL EXPERTISE.

BUT IT DOES MEAN THAT TTRPGS ARE THERAPEUTIC AND BORROW THEIR STRUCTURE FROM PSYCHOANALYTIC MODELS.

AS TIME WENT ON, EARLY MODERN TABLETOP GAMES ACTUALLY BEGAN TO RESEMBLE ANCIENT GAMES IN THAT THEY FUNCTIONED ON TWO LEVELS: TO HAVE FUN AND TO INSTRUCT.

WE'RE GETTING CLOSE NOW TO THE POINT WHERE TTRPGS START TO RESEMBLE WHAT WE SEE TODAY.

BOSTON, MASSACHUSETTS
1822

WHILE THE GAMES WE'RE ABOUT TO SEE FUNCTIONED ON TWO LEVELS, TO HAVE FUN AND TO INSTRUCT, THEY ALSO TOOK A PAGE FROM JACOB MORENO: ROLEPLAYING.

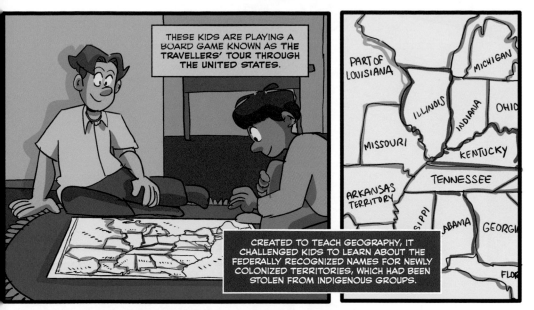

THESE KIDS ARE PLAYING A BOARD GAME KNOWN AS **THE TRAVELLERS' TOUR THROUGH THE UNITED STATES.**

PART OF LOUISIANA

MICHIGAN

ILLINOIS

INDIANA

OHIO

MISSOURI

KENTUCKY

TENNESSEE

ARKANSAS TERRITORY

SIPPI

ALABAMA

GEORGI

FLOR

CREATED TO TEACH GEOGRAPHY, IT CHALLENGED KIDS TO LEARN ABOUT THE FEDERALLY RECOGNIZED NAMES FOR NEWLY COLONIZED TERRITORIES, WHICH HAD BEEN STOLEN FROM INDIGENOUS GROUPS.

IT WAS TECHNICALLY THE FIRST BOARD GAME TO BE PRODUCED IN THE UNITED STATES.

IS THIS LOUISIANA?

WELL DONE—THAT'S CORRECT.

A LOT OF EARLY TABLETOP GAMES—AMERICAN AND BRITISH GAMES IN PARTICULAR—WERE LIKE THIS. DIDACTIC NOT JUST WITH ACADEMIC SUBJECTS, BUT ON "PROPER" MORAL RECTITUDE.

THIS GAME IS CALLED **THE MANSION OF HAPPINESS.**

CONSIDERED TO BE THE PROGENITOR OF AMERICAN BOARD GAMES, IT WAS INTRODUCED FROM BRITAIN IN 1802, BUT RERELEASED IN 1843. IT WAS THE BEST-SELLING BOARD GAME OF ITS TIME.

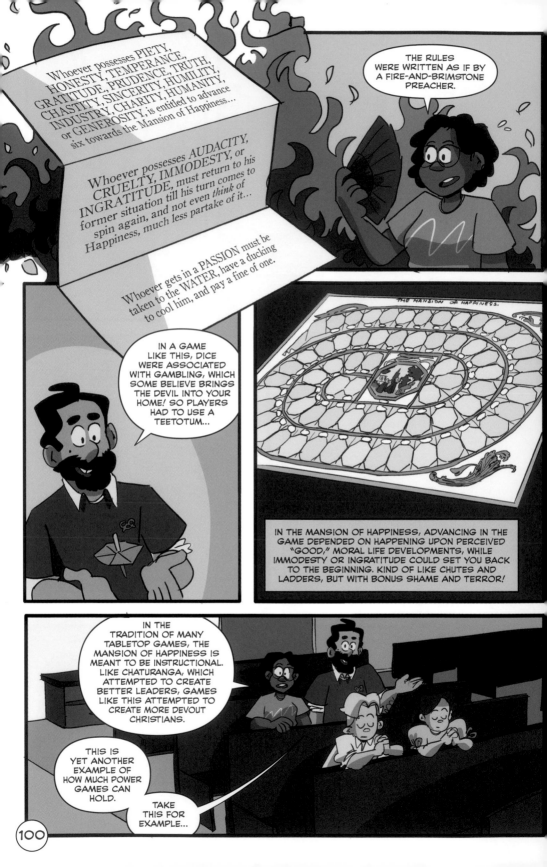

Whoever possesses PIETY, HONESTY, TEMPERANCE, GRATITUDE, PRUDENCE, TRUTH, CHASTITY, SINCERITY, HUMILITY, INDUSTRY, CHARITY, HUMANITY, or GENEROSITY, is entitled to advance six towards the Mansion of Happiness...

Whoever possesses AUDACITY, CRUELTY, IMMODESTY, or INGRATITUDE, must return to his former situation till his turn comes to spin again, and not even *think* of Happiness, much less partake of it...

Whoever gets in a PASSION must be taken to the WATER, have a ducking to cool him, and pay a fine of one.

THE RULES WERE WRITTEN AS IF BY A FIRE-AND-BRIMSTONE PREACHER.

IN A GAME LIKE THIS, DICE WERE ASSOCIATED WITH GAMBLING, WHICH SOME BELIEVE BRINGS THE DEVIL INTO YOUR HOME! SO PLAYERS HAD TO USE A TEETOTUM...

THE MANSION OF HAPPINESS.

IN THE MANSION OF HAPPINESS, ADVANCING IN THE GAME DEPENDED ON HAPPENING UPON PERCEIVED "GOOD," MORAL LIFE DEVELOPMENTS, WHILE IMMODESTY OR INGRATITUDE COULD SET YOU BACK TO THE BEGINNING. KIND OF LIKE CHUTES AND LADDERS, BUT WITH BONUS SHAME AND TERROR!

IN THE TRADITION OF MANY TABLETOP GAMES, THE MANSION OF HAPPINESS IS MEANT TO BE INSTRUCTIONAL. LIKE CHATURANGA, WHICH ATTEMPTED TO CREATE BETTER LEADERS, GAMES LIKE THIS ATTEMPTED TO CREATE MORE DEVOUT CHRISTIANS.

THIS IS YET ANOTHER EXAMPLE OF HOW MUCH POWER GAMES CAN HOLD.

TAKE THIS FOR EXAMPLE...

THE GAME OF **POPE AND PAGAN** CAME TO THE UNITED STATES IN 1844. MADE FOR PROTESTANTS, ITS MECHANICS WERE STRUCTURED AROUND A "CHRISTIAN ARMY" OF MISSIONARIES WHOSE GOAL WAS TO LAY SIEGE TO THE "STRONGHOLD OF SATAN," THE STRONGHOLD BEING ANYONE WHO EITHER FOLLOWED THE POPE (CATHOLICS) OR WAS PAGAN.

THE MISSIONARIES STARTED WITH FIFTEEN BOARD PIECES, WHILE THE POPE AND PAGAN HAD ONE.

MISSIONARIES COULD ONLY MOVE ON PATHS PAINTED IN GREEN AND LABELED WITH WORDS LIKE "KINDNESS" AND "PURITY."

THE GAME OF POPE AND PAGAN.

THE GOAL OF THE MISSIONARIES WAS TO TRAP THE POPE AND PAGAN IN A CORNER. THE POPE AND PAGAN COULD MEANWHILE CAPTURE THE MISSIONARIES.

THE ROOTS OF THIS GAME CAME FROM PROTESTANT AMERICANS ALARMED ABOUT AN INFLUX OF CATHOLIC EUROPEANS INTO AMERICA.

IN A SENSE, THIS WAS A WARGAME... OVER THE IDEA OF SAVING SOULS.

IT'S EASY TO SEE HOW GAMES IN GENERAL CAN BE INSTRUCTIONAL AND ATTEMPT TO EDUCATE IN WAYS BOTH POSITIVE AND NEGATIVE.

THIS DOESN'T MEAN THAT EVERYONE WILL BUY IN, BUT IT DOES SHOW THAT GAMES CAN BE POWERFUL TOOLS OF PERSUASION.

AFTER THE INDUSTRIAL REVOLUTION, CAPITALISM HAD BECOME THE MAIN SOCIAL DRIVER OF US SOCIETY.

IF THE MANSION OF HAPPINESS AND THE GAME OF POPE AND PAGAN REFLECTED PREINDUSTRIAL AMERICA, THE GAMES THAT FOLLOWED REFLECTED AN INDUSTRIAL ONE.

THE CHECKERED GAME OF LIFE WAS PUBLISHED IN 1860. AN INSPIRATION FOR MONOPOLY, IT BUILT ON THE BOARD FOR THE MANSION OF HAPPINESS WHILE CHANGING THE FOCUS OF SUCCESS FROM BEING A GOOD CHRISTIAN TO EARNING MONEY AND ACQUIRING ASSETS.

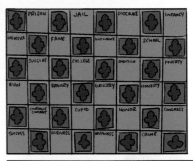

MORAL GUIDELINES WERE STILL ENCOURAGED, INCLUDING MATRIMONY, BUT EVEN THAT WAS CONFLATED WITH MONETARY SUCCESS.

PITFALLS INCLUDED GAMBLING, POVERTY, FINANCIAL RUIN, AND EVEN SUICIDE—THE ULTIMATE PUNISHMENT FOR A LIFE MISSPENT, ACCORDING TO THE GAME.

BUT A HUNDRED YEARS LATER, IN 1960, THIS GAME WAS REINVENTED AND EVENTUALLY BECAME A POPULAR AMERICAN MAINSTAY... THE GAME OF LIFE!

GAMES LIKE LIFE COME UP A LITTLE SHORT ON REPRESENTING ACTUAL LIFE, SIMILAR TO THE WAY CHATURANGA COULDN'T SIMULATE REAL WARFARE.

BUT AROUND THE SAME TIME LIFE WAS CREATED, SOME TABLETOP GAMES CAME A LOT CLOSER TO SIMULATING ACTUAL LIFE! THEY CAME FAR, FAR CLOSER TO WHAT WE NOW UNDERSTAND TO BE TTRPGS.

ALSO, THEY'RE THE KIND OF GAMES I WOULD PLAY!

NEW YORK CITY, NEW YORK, USA
1930S

THESE SWANKY GENTLEFOLK ARE PLAYING A PARLOR GAME CALLED **MR. REE!: THE FIRESIDE DETECTIVE.**

· MR ·

PERRIN

MAID

BEATRICE

MISS

LEE

NIECE

RHODA

CREATED IN 1937, THIS GAME HAD EACH PLAYER ASSUME THE ROLE OF A CHARACTER ON THE BOARD.

EACH PLAYER/CHARACTER HAD TO INTERACT WITH OTHER CHARACTERS, WHILE CHOOSING AND CONCEALING WEAPONS TO COMMIT A CRIME WITH—OR SIMPLY AVOID BEING KILLED THEMSELVES.

ONE PERSON PLAYED MR. REE, THE DETECTIVE, INTERROGATING, SNOOPING, AND ASKING TOUGH QUESTIONS.

IT SOUNDS A LOT LIKE CLUE ON ITS SURFACE. BUT WHILE IT INSPIRED CLUE, THIS GAME ISN'T BASED AROUND ONE-DIMENSIONAL CHARACTER TOKENS. IT'S ABOUT ACTING OUT THE ROLE OF YOUR CHARACTER TO ACCUSE OTHERS OR TAKE SUSPICION OFF OF YOURSELF.

I ASSURE YOU, MR. REE, I'M A STUDENT OF ERICH HECKEL, NOT SOME MURDEROUS THUG.

ANYONE CAN BECOME A MURDERER, GEORGE, UNDER THE CORRECT CIRCUMSTANCES.

GAMES LIKE THIS CAN BE LOOKED AT AS EARLY TTRPGS. THEY DON'T RELY ON STATISTICS ROLLING. BUT THEY DO FEATURE A KIND OF ROLEPLAYING FAMILIAR TO US TODAY.

EACH SESSION IS TURNED INTO A STORYTELLING EXPERIENCE THAT CHANGES EVERY TIME YOU PLAY.

I NOTICE THERE'S AN AWFUL LOT OF RED ON YOUR PALETTE...BLOOD RED...THE COLOR OF MURDER...

IT'S— IT'S FOR A BED OF PEONIES I'M PAINTING!

ANOTHER GAME LIKE THIS WAS **THE JURY BOX.**

IT ALSO CAME OUT IN 1937 AND INVOLVED PLAYING THE ROLE OF EITHER A DISTRICT ATTORNEY OR MEMBERS OF A JURY.

THE JURY MEMBERS HAD TO LISTEN TO THE DA RECOUNT THE CASE AND WERE NOT ALLOWED TO INTERRUPT. AFTERWARD, THEY COULD WRITE DOWN THEIR SUGGESTED SOLUTIONS.

AND NOW I PRESENT EVIDENCE IN THE CASE OF THE *STATE VERSUS JAMES PLATT.*

AFTER COLLECTING ALL THE SOLUTIONS, THE VERDICT WAS READ BY THE DA.

AND THE COURT FINDS THE DEFENDANT...

GUILTY!

YES!

JURY BOX IS A GAME THAT ATTEMPTS TO INSTRUCT THROUGH SIMULATION, WITH AN ADDED DASH OF ROLEPLAYING. THOUGH THE PERSON ACTING AS DA HAD A SUPPLIED STORY, THEY STILL HAD TO ASSUME CHARACTER FOR THE ROLE. THE JUROR POSITIONS WERE LESS ACTIVE, SIMULATING THE PROCESS OF BEING IN AN ACTUAL COURTROOM.

I'D DO WELL ON A REAL JURY, I MEASURE.

IT'S JUST A GAME!

TO THE 1950S?

TO THE 1950S!

RAND CORPORATION, SANTA MONICA

1957

SOON ENOUGH, THIS NEW BREED OF ROLEPLAYING GAMES DREW THE INTEREST OF BOTH THE MILITARY AND THE FBI.

IN 1957, RAND RESEARCHERS CONNECTED WITH TWO PROFESSORS AT NORTHWESTERN UNIVERSITY WHO HAD CREATED **THE INTER-NATION SIMULATION** FOR TEACHING PURPOSES.

THEIR GOAL WAS TO COMBINE WARGAMES WITH ROLEPLAYING, SO A SERIES OF IMPROVISED, REAL-WORLD SCENARIOS COULD TAKE PLACE.

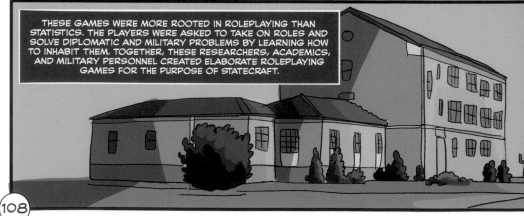

THESE GAMES WERE MORE ROOTED IN ROLEPLAYING THAN STATISTICS. THE PLAYERS WERE ASKED TO TAKE ON ROLES AND SOLVE DIPLOMATIC AND MILITARY PROBLEMS BY LEARNING HOW TO INHABIT THEM. TOGETHER, THESE RESEARCHERS, ACADEMICS, AND MILITARY PERSONNEL CREATED ELABORATE ROLEPLAYING GAMES FOR THE PURPOSE OF STATECRAFT.

WHEN PSYCHOLOGICAL STUDIES THROUGH ROLEPLAYING CAPTURED THE GOVERNMENT'S INTEREST, THEY CHANNELED IT THROUGH ITS ORGANIZATIONS. INCLUDING THE FBI.

BACK UP! I HAVE A GUN!

EASY, NOW. WE'VE GOT YOUR WIFE ON THE WAY.

ROLEPLAYING EXERCISES BECAME A MAINSTAY OF TRAINING AT COMPLEXES LIKE QUANTICO, TO PREPARE OFFICERS FOR FIELDWORK.

THESE GOVERNMENT RESEARCH GROUPS ARE STILL USING ROLEPLAYING TO THIS DAY.

BUT THE GAMING COMMUNITY WAS *ALSO* EMBRACING ROLEPLAYING AT THIS TIME.

IN 1959 A MAJOR DEVELOPMENT TOOK PLACE IN THE NONGOVERNMENTAL GAMING WORLD. **DIPLOMACY.**

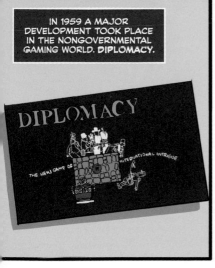

DIPLOMACY

THE NEW GAME OF INTERNATIONAL INTRIGUE

CREATED BY ALLAN B. CALHAMER IN 1954 AND RELEASED IN 1959, DIPLOMACY IS NOTABLE BECAUSE IT A) WAS NOT PLAYED WITH DICE AND B) WAS THE FIRST COMMERCIAL GAME TO BE PLAYED BY MAIL.

LIKE WITH INTER-NATION SIMULATION, THE GAME CONCERNED ITSELF WITH NEGOTIATION AND SPLITTING OFF INTO GROUPS TO ACHIEVE COLLECTIVE GOALS.

PLAYERS CREATED ELABORATE PERSONAS, WHICH APPEARED IN THE PAGES OF FAN ZINES IN THE FORM OF PLAYER PROPAGANDA, NEGOTIATIONS, AND ULTIMATUMS, IN REFERENCE TO ONGOING GAMES.

FREDONIA

#11   "SPRING 1904"   14-OCT-'64

AUSTRO-ITALIAN ALLIANCE PRESSES TURKS

CAMELOT (CP): ENGLAND WISHES PUBLICLY TO ANNOUNCE THAT THE ATTACK ON GERMANY'S SWEDEN WAS NOT AN ENGLISH ATTACK. IT WAS THE WORK OF MUTINEERS.

"'TIS WAR, RED WAR, I'LL GIVE YOU THEN,
WAR TILL MY SINEWS FAIL;
FOR A WRONG YOU HAVE DONE TO A CHIEF OF MEN,
AND A THIEF OF THE ZUKKA KHEYL." — KIPLING

NEW POSTAL DIPLOMACY ANNOUNCED

FIVE POSTAL DIPLOMACY GAMES ARE CURRENTLY IN PROGRESS:
1963B (RURITANIA)
1964A (GRAUSTARK)
1964B (FREDONIA)
1964C (BROBDINGNAG)
1964D (TRANTOR)
THE FIRST TWO ARE ON THE POINT OF COMPLETION, AND DAVE (GM 1963B) HAS ANNOUNCED A NEW G TO BEGIN SOON.

THE FEE IS $2.00

CHECK OUT THIS FANZINE WE FOUND!

GAMES OF STRATEGY

DIPLOMACY WAS PUT OUT BY AVALON HILL, PURVEYOR OF AMERICA'S FIRST WARGAMES.

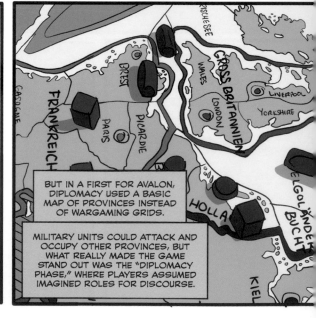

BUT IN A FIRST FOR AVALON, DIPLOMACY USED A BASIC MAP OF PROVINCES INSTEAD OF WARGAMING GRIDS.

MILITARY UNITS COULD ATTACK AND OCCUPY OTHER PROVINCES, BUT WHAT REALLY MADE THE GAME STAND OUT WAS THE "DIPLOMACY PHASE," WHERE PLAYERS ASSUMED IMAGINED ROLES FOR DISCOURSE.

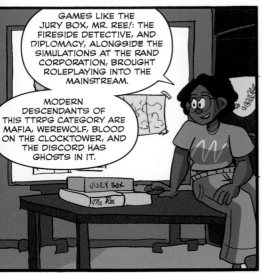

GAMES LIKE THE JURY BOX, MR. REE!: THE FIRESIDE DETECTIVE, AND DIPLOMACY, ALONGSIDE THE SIMULATIONS AT THE RAND CORPORATION, BROUGHT ROLEPLAYING INTO THE MAINSTREAM.

MODERN DESCENDANTS OF THIS TTRPG CATEGORY ARE MAFIA, WEREWOLF, BLOOD ON THE CLOCKTOWER, AND THE DISCORD HAS GHOSTS IN IT.

JURY BOX
Mr Ree

THESE ARE MY FAVORITES. THEY DON'T INVOLVE STATISTICS ROLLING OR ELABORATE STORYLINES. ALL YOU NEED IS YOUR IMAGINATION, SOME SIMPLE RULES, AND SOME FOLKS WHO ARE WILLING TO PUT THEMSELVES IN SOMEONE ELSE'S SHOES.

CHESS

JURY BOX

ST. LOUIS
2015

HAPPY HALLOWEEN!

I'M VICTORIA. EX-MILITARY. I LOST AN EYE. IN WAR.

WELL, IT'S LOVELY TO MEET YOU VICTORIA. I'M STEPHANIE BLACKCLEAVER, AND I'M A MOM.

THAT'S ME AND KEYA IN COSTUME!

ANGUS BLACKCLEAVER OF THE WESTMINSTER BLACKCLEAVERS.

KEYA AND I WERE INVITED TO A MURDER MYSTERY PARTY WHERE WE PLAYED AN ALTERNATE VERSION OF MAFIA. WE GOT TO CREATE OUR OWN CHARACTERS, AND WE ACTED OUT THE GAME AS WE PLAYED.

WHEN I ARRIVED, I KNEW I HAD TO BE IN CHARACTER IMMEDIATELY.

AS THE NIGHT WENT ON, WE GOT TO KNOW EACH OTHER'S CHARACTERS.

GATORADE? I HAVE SOME LEFTOVER FROM THE KIDS' SOCCER PRACTICE.

PASS.

ANGUS BLACKCLEAVER OF THE WELLINGTON BLACKCLEAVERS.

A GALEBORROUGHS BLACKCLEAVER DOESN'T JUST MURDER HIS OWN WIFE!

IT WAS REALLY FUN TO PRETEND TO BE DEAD. AND THE ACCUSATIONS ABOUT MY MURDER GOT HEATED AFTER A FEW DRINKS.

THE ROLEPLAY EVEN EXTENDED TO THE REST OF THE EVENING AFTER THE GAME WAS OVER! OUR FRIEND FLEET REALLY TOOK HIS ROLE AS JASON VOORHEES VERY SERIOUSLY.

THESE SORT OF ROLEPLAYING GAMES WERE MORE EXCITING TO ME BECAUSE OF THE IMMERSION.

I DIDN'T HAVE TO USE A MINIATURE AS AN AVATAR FOR THE CHARACTER I CREATED BECAUSE I COULD JUST BE THAT CHARACTER.

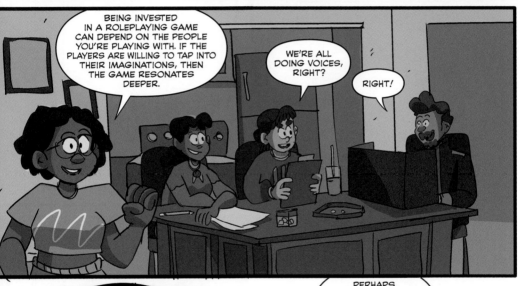

BEING INVESTED IN A ROLEPLAYING GAME CAN DEPEND ON THE PEOPLE YOU'RE PLAYING WITH. IF THE PLAYERS ARE WILLING TO TAP INTO THEIR IMAGINATIONS, THEN THE GAME RESONATES DEEPER.

WE'RE ALL DOING VOICES, RIGHT?

RIGHT!

PERHAPS THIS IS WHY SOME POINT TO TTRPGS AS CONTAINING A SENSE OF FOLIE À DEUX, OR MADNESS FOR TWO, IN FRENCH.

TECHNICALLY, FOLIE À DEUX IS A FORM OF PSYCHOSIS WHERE DELUSIONS—AND SOMETIMES FULL-OUT HALLUCINATIONS—ARE ACTUALLY SHARED BETWEEN TWO OR MORE INDIVIDUALS.

OF COURSE TTRPGS DON'T INDUCE PSYCHOSIS. PEOPLE KNOW THEY'RE USING THEIR IMAGINATIONS WHEN THEY'RE PLAYING, AND UNDERSTAND THEIR LIMITS.

BUT BOTH PLAYERS AND GMS HAVE TO BE WILLING TO INHABIT A SHARED, IMAGINED SPACE IN ORDER FOR THE GAME TO WORK. IN SHORT, TTRPGS REQUIRE TAKING PRETEND PLAY SERIOUSLY.

BACK TO DIPLOMACY—THE MOST IMPORTANT PART OF THE GAME WAS INTERPERSONAL COMMUNICATION.

SINCE BATTLES WERE BASED ON BRUTE POWER AND NOT STATISTICS ROLLING, WINNING DEPENDED ON FORMING ALLIANCES, WHICH REQUIRED BELIEVABLE ROLEPLAYING.

WARGAMERS—MANY OF WHOM ENJOYED TINKERING WITH RULES AND CONVENTIONS TO MAKE THEIR HOBBY MORE EXCITING—BEGAN TO CREATE THEIR OWN ALTERNATIVE VERSIONS OF DIPLOMACY, FEATURING LOCALES FROM TOLKIEN'S MIDDLE-EARTH OR VAST SCIENCE FICTION SPACE EMPIRES.

Mordor will not be moved by paltry threats from Rohan.

We threaten Mordor because all efforts to negotiate have proven ineffective. For the sovereignty of our people, we attack.

DURING THIS TIME, THERE WAS ALSO A BOOM OF SCIENCE FICTION/FANTASY FAN CULTURE IN LOS ANGELES AND THE BAY AREA, ONE THAT WAS BECOMING UNPRECEDENTEDLY ORGANIZED.

THIS RISE WOULD FEED INTO THE AVALANCHE OF INFLUENCES THAT PRODUCED MODERN TTRPGS.

OOH, DOES THIS MEAN WE'RE HEADING TO LA?

YUP!

LA MID 1950s

SCI-FI FANDOM GROUPS COULD BE FOUND AS EARLY AS THE 1930S IN LOS ANGELES, WHERE WRITERS LIKE LARRY NIVEN, RAY BRADBURY, AND FRITZ LIEBER CONGREGATED. THIS WOULD EVENTUALLY TRANSFORM INTO THE LOS ANGELES SCIENCE FANTASY SOCIETY (LASFS) IN THE 1950S.

WHAT MADE LASFS DIFFERENT FROM OTHER GROUPS LIKE IT WAS ORGANIZATION.

FILLED WITH DEDICATED FANS WHO MET REGULARLY, CONDITIONS WERE PERFECT FOR SOMTHING LIKE **COVENTRY** TO BLOOM.

I HOPE THE PICTURE TURNS OUT NICE!

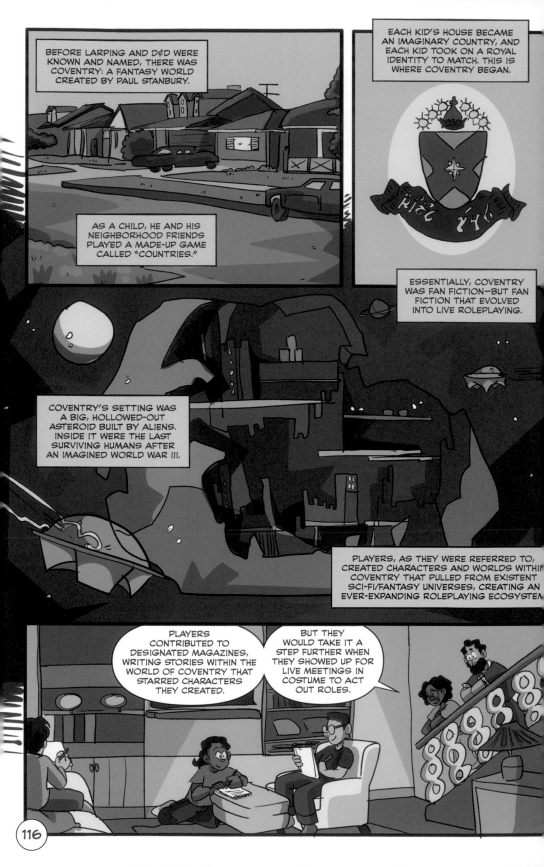

BEFORE LARPING AND D&D WERE KNOWN AND NAMED, THERE WAS COVENTRY: A FANTASY WORLD CREATED BY PAUL STANBURY.

AS A CHILD, HE AND HIS NEIGHBORHOOD FRIENDS PLAYED A MADE-UP GAME CALLED "COUNTRIES."

EACH KID'S HOUSE BECAME AN IMAGINARY COUNTRY, AND EACH KID TOOK ON A ROYAL IDENTITY TO MATCH. THIS IS WHERE COVENTRY BEGAN.

ESSENTIALLY, COVENTRY WAS FAN FICTION—BUT FAN FICTION THAT EVOLVED INTO LIVE ROLEPLAYING.

COVENTRY'S SETTING WAS A BIG, HOLLOWED-OUT ASTEROID BUILT BY ALIENS. INSIDE IT WERE THE LAST SURVIVING HUMANS AFTER AN IMAGINED WORLD WAR III.

PLAYERS, AS THEY WERE REFERRED TO, CREATED CHARACTERS AND WORLDS WITHIN COVENTRY THAT PULLED FROM EXISTENT SCI-FI/FANTASY UNIVERSES, CREATING AN EVER-EXPANDING ROLEPLAYING ECOSYSTEM.

PLAYERS CONTRIBUTED TO DESIGNATED MAGAZINES, WRITING STORIES WITHIN THE WORLD OF COVENTRY THAT STARRED CHARACTERS THEY CREATED.

BUT THEY WOULD TAKE IT A STEP FURTHER WHEN THEY SHOWED UP FOR LIVE MEETINGS IN COSTUME TO ACT OUT ROLES.

THOUGH COVENTRY DIDN'T EVEN INVOLVE GAME PLAY LIKE DIPLOMACY, WHERE THERE WERE SET GOALS, IT WAS CALLED A GAME.

THE PRIME OF RULE OF WHICH WAS USING ROLEPLAYING TO EXPAND AN IMAGINARY WORLD.

COVENTRY CAME TO AN END UNDER DARK CIRCUMSTANCES.

DUE TO SOME PLAYERS TAKING THE GAME TOO SERIOUSLY, THE CHAIR OF COVENTRY INTRODUCED A CHARACTER CALLED THE GUARDIAN TO KEEP PLAYERS IN CHECK.

THE GUARDIAN ENFORCED MORE STRINGENT RULES, LEADING TO SOME UNSTABLE PLAYERS ACTING OUT...RESULTING IN AN ACTUAL FIRE BOMB BEING THROWN ON ONE PLAYER'S LAWN.

AS YOU MIGHT EXPECT, THE GROUP FELL APART AFTER THAT.

AND A BAD TASTE WAS LEFT IN THE MOUTHS OF ALL ITS FORMER PARTICIPANTS, WHO RARELY SPOKE OF COVENTRY AFTERWARD.

BUT DESPITE ALL THAT, THE GAME USED THE SAME KIND OF COLLABORATIVE STORYTELLING THAT MADE ITS WAY INTO DUNGEONS & DRAGONS.

117

ONE OF THE THINGS YOU MIGHT NOTICE BY THIS POINT IS THAT THE EVOLUTION OF THESE GAMES ISN'T LINEAR.

INFLUENCES COME TOGETHER FROM DIFFERENT PLACES IN SOCIETY, AND IDEAS ARE EXCHANGED, OFTEN SUBCONSCIOUSLY.

AS WE'LL SOON SEE, THE KING OF MODERN TTRPGS, DUNGEONS & DRAGONS, WASN'T BORN OUT OF NOTHING IN 1974.

IN FACT, ITS COCREATOR GARY GYGAX HIMSELF NOT ONLY PLAYED COVENTRY BUT ALSO DIPLOMACY AND A WHOLE HOST OF WARGAMES.

BUT BY THE EARLY 1960S, THERE WAS STILL A GOOD AMOUNT OF MAINSTREAM SEPARATION BETWEEN THE WARGAMING COMMUNITIES AND THOSE WHO PLAYED GAMES LIKE DIPLOMACY.

AND EVEN WHEN IT CAME TO DIPLOMACY, THE JURY BOX, AND OTHERS LIKE IT, THERE WAS STILL SOMETHING MISSING FROM THE MODERN TTRPG EQUATION.

SOMETHING THAT WOULD BRING TOGETHER ROLEPLAYING AND STATISTICS.

TTRPGS BECAME MY GATEWAY TO CREATIVITY. WEEKENDS SPENT PLAYING D&D BLED INTO MY BOOKSHELF. I COULDN'T GET ENOUGH!

YOU SHOULDN'T READ SO MUCH OF THAT FANTASY CRAP. WHY DON'T YOU READ SOMETHING THAT TAKES PLACE IN THE REAL WORLD?

EH. I'LL PASS.

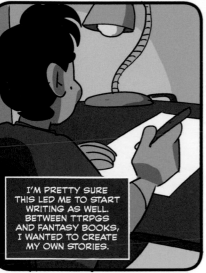

I'M PRETTY SURE THIS LED ME TO START WRITING AS WELL. BETWEEN TTRPGS AND FANTASY BOOKS, I WANTED TO CREATE MY OWN STORIES.

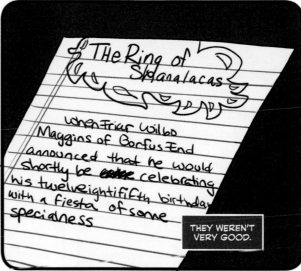

The Ring of Skalanalacas

when Friar Wilbo Maggins of Gorfus End announced that he would shortly be ~~eate~~ celebrating his twelveightififth birthday with a fiesta of some specialness

THEY WEREN'T VERY GOOD.

I DREW MAPS, TRIED TO CREATE NEW LANGUAGES.

VISBLAGHARFARK TO'LOKIAR FARU!

AND I DREW LOTS OF DRAGONS.

BUT IT WAS DIFFERENT WITH ROLEPLAYING GAMES.

WHEN IT CAME TO THEM, THE VERY CONCEPT OF STORY TOOK ON NEW DIMENSIONS.

YOU REALLY WANT TO STEAL THE FISH? JUST GO AHEAD AND TRY IT.

I THINK I WILL.

I ALSO WOULD LIKE TO STEAL A FISH.

WE CONSTANTLY PUSHED THE GM'S BUTTONS, ALWAYS THROWING HIS PREDETERMINED CAMPAIGN OFF COURSE.

YOU'RE JUST COPYING ME!

SO YOU'RE THE ONLY ONE ALLOWED TO STEAL FISH?

WELL, I AM A THIEF, UNLIKE YOU, LAWFUL GOOD *PALADIN*.

BUT I WAS ALSO IMPRESSED BY HOW THE GM REACTED.

YOU'VE STOLEN THE FISH SUCCESSFULLY. BUT ALTHOUGH YOU WEREN'T SEEN BY THE FISHMONGER...

YOUR ACTIONS DIDN'T GO UNNOTICED...

OH CRAP.

YOU FEEL A HAND ON YOUR SHOULDER AND TURN AROUND TO SEE A KNIGHT IN SILVER ARMOR, WEARING THE SIGIL OF THE TRUTH GUILD.

MY CHARACTER'S HISTORY PROFICIENCY SHOULD BE ABLE TO IDENTIFY THAT GUILD.

IT'S A KNIGHTLY ORDER. PALADINS.

WE CAN'T HAVE OUR PALADIN KNIGHTS STEALING IN BROAD DAYLIGHT. IT WILL BRING RUIN TO OUR ORDER.

RETURN WHAT YOU'VE TAKEN.

ACTION SUCCESSFUL!

HEY!

BACKUP!

I WASN'T SURE WHETHER OUR GM HAD PLANNED FOR THE PALADIN OR WHETHER IT WAS SOMETHING HE CAME UP WITH ON THE FLY. BUT THE STORY ENDED UP GOING IN A DIFFERENT DIRECTION, ALL DUE TO STEALING A FISH.

AS I GREW OLDER AND GM'ED MY OWN GAMES, I FOUND THAT LEADING THEM REQUIRED BOTH PREPARATION AND IMPROV.

I HAD SOME CONTINGENCY PLANS FOR WHEN PLAYERS DID SOMETHING UNEXPECTED. OTHERS, I JUST IMPROVISED TO THE BEST OF MY ABILITY.

EVENTUALLY, I LEARNED THAT STORIES IN TTRPGS ARE NEVER SET IN STONE, EVEN THE ONES THAT ACCOUNT FOR MYRIAD POSSIBILITIES.

BECAUSE PLAYERS HAVE AGENCY, STORYTELLING BECOMES COMMUNAL, WHERE EVERYONE CAN SHARE IN HOW IT PLAYS OUT.

YOU FELT LIKE THE STORY WAS ALIVE.

AND COMMUNAL!

THIS IS A PRODUCT OF COLLECTIVE STORYTELLING. TTRPGS ARE SPECIAL IN THAT PLAYERS GAIN THE ABILITY TO BECOME THE PROTAGONIST OR ANTAGONIST.

IT BRINGS THE IDEA OF IDENTIFYING WITH CHARACTERS TO A WHOLE DIFFERENT LEVEL.

A LEVEL THAT BRINGS US CLOSER TO UNDERSTANDING WHAT TTRPGS ARE ALL ABOUT.

PUPPETRY

NAUMACHIA

SO TO RECAP, EARLY RITUAL DRAMAS GAVE WAY TO HISTORICAL REENACTMENT.

SOME PEOPLE PUSHED HISTORICAL REENACTMENT TOO FAR, SO THAT IT CULMINATED IN DISPLAYS LIKE NAUMACHIA.

ON THE BOARD GAME END OF THINGS, GAMES LIKE CHATURANGA LED TO CHESS...WHICH THEN LED TO KRIEGSPIEL.

AS WARGAMES ADVANCED ON THEIR OWN INDEPENDENT TRACK, PERFORMANCE ART LIKE COMMEDIA DELL'ARTE OFFERED A SAFE, CONTROLLED ENVIRONMENT FOR AUDIENCE PARTICIPANTS TO AFFECT THE OUTCOME OF STORIES AND FOR ACTORS TO IMPROVISE ACCORDINGLY.

JACOB L. MORENO'S PSYCHODRAMA, WHERE THE TERM ROLEPLAYING WAS COINED, WOULD COME TO DESCRIBE INTERACTIVE THEATER THAT COULD BE USED TO PRODUCE THERAPEUTIC RESULTS.

BOARD GAMES EMERGING DURING THAT PERIOD OF EVOLVING SOCIAL SCIENCE INCLUDED THE JURY BOX AND MR. REE!: THE FIRESIDE DETECTIVE— WHICH INVOLVED ROLEPLAYING.

GOVERNMENTS FACILITATED THE WIDESPREAD PRACTICE OF ROLEPLAYING EXERCISES IN THEIR INSTITUTIONS, COLLABORATING WITH ACADEMIC CIRCLES PREOCCUPIED WITH PSYCHOLOGY AND SOCIAL SCIENCES.

INTER-NATION SIMULATION GAMES WERE THE RESULT, AND THINGS LIKE IT ARE STILL USED TO THIS DAY.

ALL OF THESE FORCES WERE COLLUDING TO CREATE MODERN TTRPGS.

BUT A CRUCIAL ELEMENT WAS NECESSARY TO CREATE THE GAME THAT *POPULARIZED* MODERN TTRPGS.

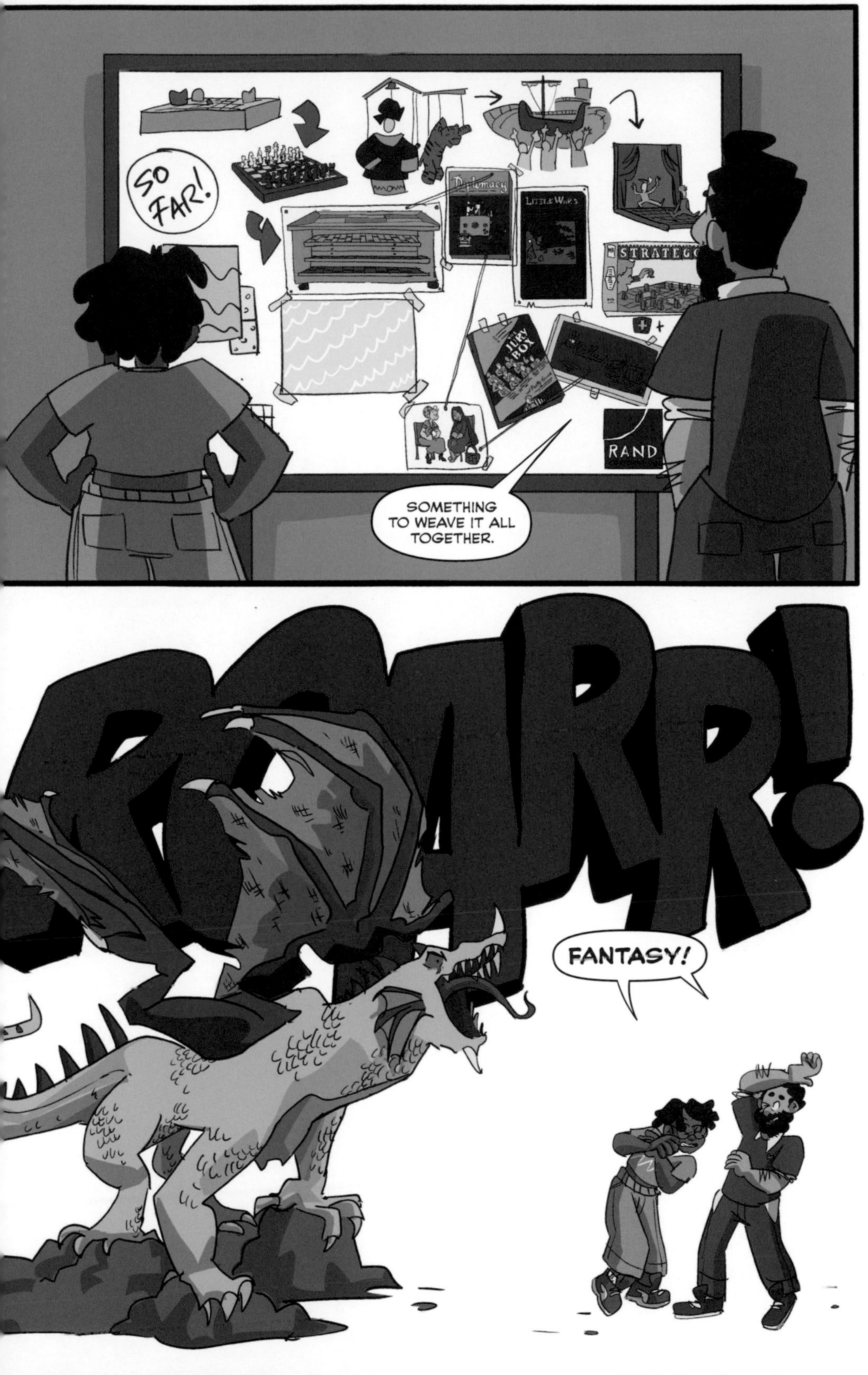
SO FAR!
Diplomacy
LITTLE WARS
STRATEGO
JURY BOX
RAND
SOMETHING TO WEAVE IT ALL TOGETHER.
ROARR!
FANTASY!

Part Five

MAGIC IN THE MODERN WORLD

LAKE GENEVA, WISCONSIN, USA
1968

THESE BASEMENT-DWELLING FOLKS ARE PLAYING A GAME THEY CAME UP WITH CALLED THE SIEGE OF BODENBURG.

SIEGE OF BODENBERG

SW - SUPPLY WAGON
L - LANSQUENETS
K - MOUNTED KNIGHTS
H - MOUNTED HUNS
AT - ATTACKER'S FOOT MEN

IT WAS CREATED BY A MAN NAMED HENRY BODENSTEDT AND IS KNOWN AS ONE OF THE EARLIEST MEDIEVAL WARGAMES.

AMONG THE GROUP WAS A HOBBY GAMER AND GAME DESIGNER: GARY GYGAX.

AND THIS IS DAVE ARNESON, WHO WAS ALSO A HOBBY GAMER AND GAME DESIGNER.

MEDIEVAL WARGAMING IS *TOTALLY* BETTER THAN NAPOLEONIC WARGAMING.

DON'T YOU THINK, GARY?

YEAH SURE, IT'S FUN. BUT WHAT IF WE TOOK IT ALL JUST A STEP FURTHER?

WE CAN TAKE SOME OF THIS STUFF...

AND A LITTLE BIT OF THAT...

CASTLES

EXPERIENCE POINTS, LEVELS, CHARACTER TRAITS...

AND HEAR ME OUT FOR A SEC. WHAT IF WE TAKE THE WHOLE *CONAN THE BARBARIAN* SHTICK AND STAGE GAMES IN DUNGEONS?

AND WE'LL CALL IT DUNGEONS *AND* DRAGONS.

GREAT! GOOD!

SUCCESS

OKAY, SO THE CREATION OF D&D DIDN'T HAPPEN EXACTLY THAT WAY. BUT YOU GET THE POINT.

GARY GYGAX AND DAVE ARNESON WERE LONGTIME STAPLES OF THE WARGAMING COMMUNITY.

THEY NOT ONLY PLAYED EVERYTHING THERE WAS TO PLAY, BUT CONSTANTLY ALTERED EXISTING GAMES TO MAKE THEM MORE EXCITING. THEY WERE ALSO COMMUNITY BUILDERS, ALLOWING THE TINY WORLD OF WARGAMING TO SURVIVE, PARTICULARLY IN THE UNITED STATES.

ARNESON WAS A GENIUS OF INNOVATION. HE INCORPORATED FANTASY ENVIRONMENTS INTO GAMES IN DYNAMIC WAY.

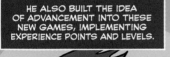

HE ALSO BUILT THE IDEA OF ADVANCEMENT INTO THESE NEW GAMES, IMPLEMENTING EXPERIENCE POINTS AND LEVELS.

EXPERIENCE POINTS (XP)
0 → 300 → 900
LEVELS
PROFICIENCY
BONUSES!

BOTH ARNESON AND GYGAX BORROWED FROM OTHER GAMES AND GAME DESIGNERS LIKE DAVID WESELY AND TONY BATH. BUT IF WE COVERED ALL OF THESE FOLKS, WE WOULDN'T BE GIVING YOU A SIDE QUEST, BUT A FULL-ON SAGA OF INFORMATION! BUT KNOW THAT WITHOUT THEM, D&D WOULDN'T HAVE COME ABOUT.

TO PUT IT MILDLY, BOTH GYGAX AND ARNESON WERE BIG SCI-FI/FANTASY ENTHUSIASTS.

INFLUENCED BY THE WORKS OF J.R.R. TOLKIEN, ROBERT E. HOWARD, FRITZ LEIBER, JACK VANCE, AND OTHERS, THE DUO SET OUT TO INTRODUCE FANTASY INTO WARGAMING.

THOUGH IT'S ALSO WORTH POINTING OUT THAT DESPITE HIS HISTORICAL IMPORTANCE, GYGAX AS A PERSON WAS COMPLEX, CONTRIBUTING TO BOTH THE BEST AND WORST OF WHAT THE WORLD OF D&D WOULD OFFER THE WORLD IN TERMS OF COMMUNITY AND INCLUSION.

EXISTENT WARGAMERS DIDN'T WANT TO CHANGE THE FORMAT OF THEIR BELOVED GAMES, ROOTED IN THE NAPOLEONIC WARS.

GET OUTTA HERE, GYGAX!

THIS IS WHY OLD-SCHOOL **NAPOLEONIC WARGAMERS** CAME TO BE CALLED GROGNARDS— A NAME GIVEN TO NAPOLEON'S IMPERIAL GUARD THAT WOULD COME TO REFER TO ANY GAMER WITH OLD-FASHIONED TASTES.

GROGNARDS WOULD END UP MARGINALIZING TRADITIONAL WARGAMING.

AFTER WORLD WAR II, AMERICA EMBRACED A PRETTY EXTREME BRAND OF SOCIAL CONSERVATISM, WITH STRICT GENDER ROLES—ALL COMPOUNDED BY SEGREGATION AND ANTI-COMMUNIST FERVOR.

BUT 1960S AMERICA WAS UNDERGOING A CULTURAL REVOLUTION

AS A MASSIVE YOUTH-LED MOVEMENT SPILLED INTO THE STREETS, TRADITIONAL WARGAMERS BEGAN TO LOOK STODGY, CONSERVATIVE, AND MILITARISTIC.

WE SHALL OVER COME

WE DEMAND EQUAL RIGHTS

JUSTICE DO YOU KNOW THE MEANING

I AM A MAN

GIVE ME FREEDOM OR GIVE ME DEATH

GYGAX AND ARNESON MOSTLY GREW UP READING CONAN THE BARBARIAN, FAFHRD AND THE GRAY MOUSER, AND OTHER SUCH STORIES, MANY OF WHICH COULD BE FOUND IN THE PAGES OF PULP MAGAZINES LIKE *WEIRD TALES*.

FANTASY CAME TO OCCUPY ITS OWN DISTINCT CATEGORY FROM SCIENCE FICTION IN THE 1930S, WITH EMERGENT PULP MAGAZINES FEATURING H.P. LOVECRAFT, AUGUST W. DERLETH, ROBERT E. HOWARD, AND OTHERS.

THIS MOVED THE GENRE AWAY FROM CONSTRAINTS IMPOSED BY SCIENCE FICTION WRITERS WHO DIDN'T ALLOW STORIES INTO THEIR MAGAZINES THAT WEREN'T ANCHORED BY HARD SCIENCE.

DURING THIS TIME, CERTAIN BOOKS, FILMS, AND COMICS BECAME PART OF COUNTERCULTURE, WHETHER THEY INTENDED TO OR NOT. THIS WAS ESPECIALLY TRUE WHEN IT CAME TO THE WORKS OF OXFORD LINGUIST J.R.R. TOLKIEN.

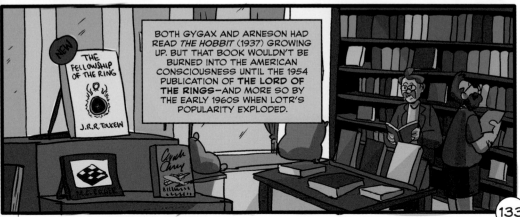

BOTH GYGAX AND ARNESON HAD READ *THE HOBBIT* (1937) GROWING UP. BUT THAT BOOK WOULDN'T BE BURNED INTO THE AMERICAN CONSCIOUSNESS UNTIL THE 1954 PUBLICATION OF **THE LORD OF THE RINGS**—AND MORE SO BY THE EARLY 1960S WHEN LOTR'S POPULARITY EXPLODED.

THERE ARE MANY REASONS FOR THIS, ONE BEING THAT TOLKIEN'S FANTASY EPIC—AND TOLKIEN HIMSELF—WAS ANTI-INDUSTRY. IN HIS BOOKS, MACHINERY, REFINERIES, AND INSTRUMENTS OF MODERN WAR WERE LOOKED UPON AS HOSTILE TOWARD NATURE, AND SO VILLAINOUS.

ANOTHER REASON FOR IDENTIFICATION AMONG HIPPIES CAME FROM THE POPULAR NOTION OF GOING ON A JOURNEY FOUND IN BOTH *THE HOBBIT* AND THE LORD OF THE RINGS.

PROVINCIAL HALFLINGS LEAVE THEIR SMALL, CLOSED-MINDED HOMETOWNS TO LEARN ABOUT THE OUTSIDE WORLD.

THESE JOURNEYS WEREN'T ALWAYS LITERAL EITHER. ANOTHER FEATURE OF THE COUNTERCULTURE REVOLUTION WAS THE USE OF PSYCHOTROPIC DRUGS TO EXPAND CONSCIOUSNESS AND BREAK FROM WHAT SOCIETY TELLS YOU YOU'RE SUPPOSED TO BE, MAN.

AND THOUGH TOLKIEN HIMSELF MIGHT HAVE BEEN HORRIFIED BY THIS, BEING A DEVOUT ROMAN CATHOLIC, HIS FANS FOUND MIDDLE-EARTH TO BE HIGHLY PSYCHEDELIC.

OVERALL, THE THEME OF A LITTLE PERSON BURDENED TO DESTROY A WEAPON OF MASS DESTRUCTION, JOINING WITH A SMALL FELLOWSHIP TO FIGHT A WAR TO END ALL WARS, AND RETURNING TO SIMPLE LIVING RESONATED WITH THE GENERATION OF ANTIWAR AND COMMUNAL LOVE.

TWAS IN THE DARKEST DEPTHS OF MORDOR!

LED ZEPPELIN, GENESIS, PEARLS BEFORE SWINE, AND BLACK SABBATH ALL HAD SONGS DIRECTLY FEATURING CHARACTERS AND THEMES FROM THE LORD OF THE RINGS.

WOO!

THE BEATLES ALMOST ADAPTED THE BOOK INTO A FILM STARRING EACH OF THEM AS CHARACTERS, BUT IT NEVER CAME TO BE.

135

THROUGHOUT ALL OF THIS, TOLKIEN BECAME AN UNWITTING HERO OF THE 1960s COUNTERCULTURE. BOTH GYGAX AND ARNESON, WHILE NOT INVOLVED IN THE HIPPY MOVEMENT, GOT CAUGHT UP IN TOLKIEN MANIA.

GYGAX'S FIRST FORAYS INTO FANTASY WARGAMING WOULD INCLUDE CREATURES FROM MIDDLE-EARTH—A TREND HE BROUGHT TO D&D AS WELL, BEFORE BEING SANCTIONED BY THE TOLKIEN ESTATE. BUT WHILE TRUE THAT TOLKIEN'S INFLUENCE CAN BE SEEN THROUGHOUT D&D, IT WASN'T THE ONLY INFLUENCE.

ENTER: CONAN THE BARBARIAN!

CREATED BY WRITER ROBERT E. HOWARD IN 1932, CONAN THE BARBARIAN (AKA CONAN THE CIMMERIAN) IS A GRUELING, GRITTY, SWORDS & SORCERY ACTION HERO WHO BULLDOZES HIS WAY THROUGH TOIL FOR THE SAKE OF BLOOD AND GLORY.

CONAN THE BARBARIAN TALES COULDN'T BE MORE DIFFERENT THAN WHAT TOLKIEN WROTE. HOWARD'S STORIES WEREN'T ONLY MORE SENSATIONAL AND BRUTAL, BUT HIS WORLD, HYBORIA, WAS AN EVIL ONE, WHERE SORCERERS USED MAGIC TO TORTURE AND SEDUCE.

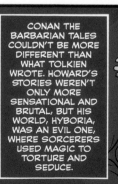

THERE WERE NO WIZENED WIZARDS IN CONAN STORIES. ONLY WICKED SPELL-SLINGERS LOCKING PEOPLE IN DUNGEONS.

CONAN WOULD THEN ERUPT INTO ACTION, DEFEAT ALL EVIL, AND TAKE THE SPOILS OF HIS BATTLE, WHICH INCLUDED NOT JUST TREASURE, BUT, EH, WOMEN.

EVEN IF THEY WERE INNOVATIVE, CONAN STORIES ARE GENERALLY CONSIDERED ABOUT AS SEXIST AS THEY COME—AND THEIR CREATOR WAS AN AVOWED RACIST. TOLKIEN'S WORK CONTAINED RACIST UNDERTONES AS WELL, BUT HOWARD'S VIEWS WERE ALMOST AS BAD AS H.P. LOVECRAFT'S.

-AMRA- 20¢

CONAN THE BARBARIAN WAS THE PROGENITOR OF THE **SWORD AND SORCERY** SUBGENRE OF FANTASY, A NAME GIVEN TO THE GENRE BY FRITZ LIEBER IN RESPONSE TO A FANZINE LETTER BY MICHAEL MOORCOCK.

By Fritz Leiber

I feel more certain than ever [that this field] should be called the sword-and-sorcery story. This accurately describes the points of culture-level and supernatural element and also immediately distinguishes it from the cloak-and-sword (historical adventure) story — and (quite incidentally) from the cloak-and-dagger (international espionage) story too! ['There are many possibilities along this line — cloak-and-mask (comic book heroes), cutlass-and-dagger (piracy), rocket-and-ray gun (space opera), and vine-and-loincloth (Tarzan).]

CONAN, WITH HIS "EXOTIC" ADVENTURES AND MORALLY COMPROMISED PERSONA, HEAVILY INFLUENCED THE CREATORS OF D&D. BUT SO DID CONAN'S SUCCESSOR, THE MORE COMPLEX ELRIC OF MELNIBONÉ BY MICHAEL MOORCOCK.

OH MY!

ELRIC FIRST APPEARED IN *SCIENCE FANTASY MAGAZINE* IN 1961. THE LAST EMPEROR OF A DECAYED ISLAND CIVILIZATION CALLED MELNIBONÉ, ELRIC WAS AN ANTIHERO LIKE CONAN, BUT ASIDE FROM THAT, THEY WERE DIFFERENT IN EVERY WAY.

LITHE AND BONE-PALE TO COUNTER CONAN'S BULK AND BRONZE, WITH CRIMSON EYES INSTEAD OF THE BARBARIAN'S VOLCANIC BLUE, ELRIC IS NOT ONLY AN OUTCAST AMONG HIS KIND, BUT IS ALSO A DRUG-ADDLED SORCERER WHO RELIES ON HIS SWORD, STORMBRINGER, TO DEVOUR SOULS TO MAINTAIN STRENGTH.

BE WARY OF THIS DEVIL BLADE, MOONGLUM. IT KILLS THE FOE—BUT SAVORS THE BLOOD OF FRIENDS AND KINFOLK MOST.

ELRIC WAS A STATEMENT AGAINST POPULAR FANTASY, NOT ONLY IN RESPONSE TO CONAN BUT IN REFUTATION OF TOLKIEN'S DUALITY OF GOOD AND EVIL.

HE WAS, AS MOORCOCK DESCRIBED HIM, A "DOOMED HERO," WHOSE POWER CAME AT A GREAT MORAL COST, INSPIRED MORE BY TRAGIC FIGURES LIKE LORD SEPULCHRAVE THAN MUSCLE-BOUND ACTION HEROES.

IMPORTANTLY, ELRIC IS ONE OF MICHAEL MOORCOCK'S ETERNAL CHAMPIONS, A SERVANT TO COSMIC BALANCE, WHICH IS WHERE THE AUTHOR'S NOTIONS OF LAW AND CHAOS EMERGED.

IF YOU'VE PLAYED DUNGEONS & DRAGONS, THEN YOU'VE LIKELY COME ACROSS LAW AND CHAOS AS TWO PARTS OF THE **ALIGNMENT** CHART. BUT IF YOU HAVEN'T, AN ALIGNMENT CHART IS A RUBRIC TO DESIGNATE A CHARACTER'S MORALS AND ETHICS.

FROM LEFT TO RIGHT TRACKS YOUR CHARACTER'S VIEW ON CIVIC LAW. AND FROM TOP TO BOTTOM, YOU HAVE A MORAL SPAN OF GOOD AND EVIL.

LAWFUL GOOD	NEUTRAL GOOD	CHAOTIC GOOD
LAWFUL NEUTRAL	TRUE NEUTRAL	CHAOTIC NEUTRAL
LAWFUL EVIL	NEUTRAL EVIL	CHAOTIC EVIL

IN THE MIDDLE OF IT ALL IS NEUTRAL, AN OUTLOOK THAT DOESN'T LEAN ONE WAY OR THE OTHER.

SO FAR!

THOUGH ELRIC'S SYSTEM OF LAW AND CHAOS WAS DEFINITELY AN INNOVATING FORCE IN POPULAR FANTASY, THE IDEA CAN BE TRACED BACK TO AUTHOR POUL ANDERSON AND HIS NOVELS INSPIRED BY NORSE FOLKLORE.

IN THOSE STORIES, GODS ARE GOVERNED BY FORCES LIKE LAW, CHAOS, FATE, DESTINY, NECESSITY, AND MORE. MOORCOCK FOUND ANDERSON'S WORK TO BE SUPERIOR TO THAT OF TOLKIEN'S.

IT SHOULD ALSO BE SAID THAT ALTHOUGH TOLKIEN'S WORLD DERIVED FROM NORSE MYTH AS WELL, HIS MORAL UNIVERSE WAS MORE CATHOLIC IN NATURE.

WHEN ALIGNMENT CHARTS FIRST ENTERED D&D, THEY WERE USED TO DIFFERENTIATE PLAYABLE **CLASSES** MORE THAN TO CREATE PERSONALITIES. YOUR ALIGNMENT DETERMINED YOUR POWERS, AND IF YOU BETRAYED YOUR ALIGNMENT, YOU COULD BE PENALIZED AND LOSE THOSE POWERS.

ALIGNMENT
CHAOTIC EVIL
RULES
DON'T BE NICE!!

EVENTUALLY, ALIGNMENT WOULD BE EXPANDED ON. RECENTLY, WIZARDS OF THE COAST DID AWAY WITH THE IDEA OF CERTAIN CREATURES BEING CLASSIFIED AS EVIL, FOR INSTANCE. THE IDEA OF EVIL RACES PARALLELS REAL-WORLD RACISM, SO REMOVING THIS WAS A STEP IN THE RIGHT DIRECTION.

IN AN ATTEMPT TO CREATE A NEW SPACE FOR WARGAMERS, GYGAX RAN THE FIRST GEN CON AT LAKE GENEVA IN 1968.

GEN CON 1968

THERE, HE PLAYED SIEGE OF BODENBURG FOR THE FIRST TIME, DESIGNED BY HENRY BODENSTEDT.

CASTLE AND CRUSADE SOCIETY

INSPIRED, GYGAX FOUNDED **THE CASTLE AND CRUSADE SOCIETY** IN 1970, WHICH WAS MOSTLY MADE UP OF WARGAMERS IN THE LAKE GENEVA AREA.

THE GOAL OF THE SOCIETY WAS TO GET GROGNARDS TO EMBRACE SETTINGS OUTSIDE OF THE NAPOLEONIC WARS.

GROGNARDS ONLY

CASTLE AND CRUSADE SOCIETY THIS WAY

DON'T GIVE UP THE SHIP RULES FOR THE GREAT AGE OF SAIL
Arneson, Gygax & Carr

SINCE THEY BECAME FRIENDS THROUGH WARGAMING AND CAME FROM SIMILAR BACKGROUNDS, IT'S EASY TO SEE HOW GARY GYGAX AND DAVE ARNESON WOULD PROGRESS TO WORKING TOGETHER ON A GAME. THE ESTABLISHMENT OF THE CASTLE & CRUSADE SOCIETY LED TO THEIR FIRST COLLABORATION. IN 1972, THEY CREATED A NAVAL WARGAME CALLED DON'T GIVE UP THE SHIP, WHICH WOULD BE PUBLISHED BY **GUIDON GAMES**.

WE SHOULD MAKE A GAME TOGETHER!

I'LL HAVE TO CHECK MY SCHEDULE.

DOMESDAY BOOK
15 APRIL 1970
#3

WHAT DID YOU PUT IN THIS DRINK YOU SAVAGE!

FOLLOWING THE GAME'S SUCCESS, THE TWO WOULD DIVE INTO FANTASY WARGAMING, BEGINNING WITH THE *DOMESDAY BOOK*.

DOMESDAY BOOK

A NEWSLETTER FOUNDED BY GYGAX IN 1970 AND PUBLISHED BY THE CASTLE AND CRUSADE SOCIETY; IT PUT OUT BULLETINS AND ARTICLES, AND SET OUT RULES FOR CONDUCTING MEDIEVAL WARGAMES, CREATING NEW STANDARDS FOR THE GROWING COMMUNITY.

EVENTUALLY, GYGAX'S EFFORTS WERE NOTICED BY GUIDON GAMES, A COMPANY WHOSE ESTABLISHMENT IN 1971 REFLECTED THE GROWING POPULARITY OF MINIATURE WARGAMING.

GUIDON GAMES ASKED GYGAX TO PRODUCE A MORE STANDARDIZED GAME THAT THEY COULD PUBLISH AND SELL.

JEFF PERREN, WHO WAS A MEMBER OF THE CASTLE & CRUSADE SOCIETY, COLLABORATED WITH GYGAX TO CREATE CHAINMAIL.

Chainmail
rules for medieval miniatures
by
Gary Gygax & Jeff Perren

GUIDON GAMES

CHAINMAIL IS A DIRECT PRECURSOR TO DUNGEONS & DRAGONS. GYGAX'S GOAL IN ITS DEVELOPMENT WAS TO CAPTURE THE FEELING OF BEING INSIDE A CONAN THE BARBARIAN BOOK.

WHICH IS WHY THE GAME INCLUDED A FANTASY SUPPLEMENT.

THIS SUPPLEMENT WAS NOTABLY FILLED WITH CREATURES FROM TOLKIEN'S WORLD, INCLUDING HOBBITS, TROLLS, BALROGS, AND DRAGONS.

GYGAX HAD AN ODD, CONTRADICTORY RELATIONSHIP WITH TOLKIEN, DENYING THAT D&D TOOK MUCH INFLUENCE FROM MIDDLE-EARTH, WHILE SIMULTANEOUSLY FOLDING MIDDLE-EARTH INTO ITS WORLD.

Fantasy
supplement

HOBBITS, SPRITES
DWARVES, GNOMES
BALROGS, OGRES
DJINN, DRAGONS
GIANTS

CHAINMAIL WOULD FEATURE ASPECTS FAMILIAR TO MODERN D&D PLAYERS.

CHAINMAIL ALSO INTRODUCED THE SAVING THROW, BORROWED FROM A GAME DEVELOPER NAMED TONY BATH.

A LOT OF RULES THAT MADE THEIR WAY INTO D&D CAME FROM BATH'S RULES FOR MEDIEVAL WARGAMES, A PAMPHLET HE PUBLISHED IN 1966.

THE SUCCESS OF THE **SAVING THROW** IN CHAINMAIL DEPENDED ON HOW STRONG THE DEFENDER'S ARMOR WAS.

THIS SET THE PRECEDENT FOR **ARMOR CLASS,** WHERE BETTER/ STRONGER ARMOR MADE IT EASIER TO DODGE AN ATTACK.

ADDITIONALLY, AND WITH THE HELP OF DAVE ARNESON'S RULES, CHAINMAIL BEGAN LEANING MORE INTO THE KIND OF ROLEPLAYING WE SEE IN MODERN TTRPGS.

USING THE BASIC RULE SYSTEM FOR CHAINMAIL'S FANTASY SUPPLEMENT, ARNESON MADE A KEY STEP TOWARD THE DEVELOPMENT OF D&D, KNOWN AS...

THE BLACKMOOR CAMPAIGN.

THE BLACKMOOR CAMPAIGN BORROWED WORLD-BUILDING ELEMENTS FROM THE LORD OF THE RINGS AND THE GOTHIC SOAP OPERA *DARK SHADOWS*.

CASTLE BLACKMODRE

TESTED WITH MEMBERS OF THE CASTLE & CRUSADE SOCIETY, BLACKMOOR ENCOURAGED CHARACTERS TO TAKE ON DIFFERENT ROLES AND OFFERED NOT ONLY MILITARY COMBAT, BUT DUNGEON EXPLORATION, WHICH ARNESON TOOK FROM HIS LOVE OF CONAN STORIES.

INTO THE DUNGEONS OF CASTLE BLACK-MOOR! WILL YOU JOIN ME?

ABSOLUTELY.

THE DUNGEON EXPLORATION FACTOR THAT ARNESON ADDED, ALONG WITH BEGINNING A QUEST AT A TAVERN (WHICH WOULD CARRY OVER TO D&D), WAS ESPECIALLY POPULAR AMONG PLAYERS.

BUT FIRST, WE FEAST!

GREETINGS, ADVENTURERS. LET ME GUESS...YOU'RE LOOKING FOR GRAGNAR'S FORTUNE?

THE BLACKMOOR CAMPAIGN IS A STUDY IN GAME EVOLUTION, GROWING OUT OF A TRADITIONAL MEDIEVAL WARGAME BUT LETTING DIFFERENT PLAYERS ESTABLISH KINGDOMS, IDENTITIES, ALLIANCES, AND GRIEVANCES. IT COMBINED TACTICAL BATTLE AND COMMUNAL STORYTELLING.

AS PLAYERS TOOK ON MORE ACTIVE CHARACTER ROLES IN THE GAME, THEY BECAME MORE INVESTED.

EVENTS IN THE CAMPAIGN BEGAN TO CIRCULATE IN A NEWS SHEET CALLED *THE BLACKMOOR GAZETTE AND RUMORMONGER*, ENHANCING CHARACTER INTERACTIONS, POLITICS, AND CAMPAIGN EVENTS.

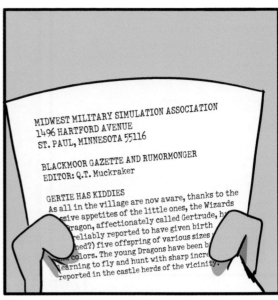

MIDWEST MILITARY SIMULATION ASSOCIATION
1496 HARTFORD AVENUE
ST. PAUL, MINNESOTA 55116

BLACKMOOR GAZETTE AND RUMORMONGER
EDITOR: Q.T. Muckraker

GERTIE HAS KIDDIES
As all in the village are now aware, thanks to the ~~ssive~~ appetites of the little ones, the Wizards ~~ragon,~~ affectionately called Gertrude, h~~ reliably reported to have given birth ~~hed?)~~ five offspring of various sizes ~~colors.~~ The young Dragons have been b~~ learning to fly and hunt with sharp incre~~ reported in the castle herds of the vicinity.

IN THE FALL OF THAT YEAR, ARNESON DEMONSTRATED THE GAME TO GYGAX, WHO WAS AMAZED. AND FROM THERE...

THE TWO BEGAN TO COLLABORATE ON WHAT WOULD BECOME DUNGEONS & DRAGONS.

IF THE WORD BLACKMOOR ITSELF SEEMS FAMILIAR, THIS IS WHY. D&D WOULD INCORPORATE IT INTO ITS UNIVERSE.

THE BLACKMOOR CAMPAIGN ALSO LED TO THE CREATION OF THE FIRST CHARACTER SHEET. THIS WAS SUBMITTED BY A FAN OF THE GAME, A PLAYER WHO HAD CREATED A SHEET FOR HIS WIZARD GAYLORD TO KEEP TRACK OF THE CHARACTER'S ATTRIBUTES.

WIZARD GAYLORD
ORGANIC TYPE
LEVEL: 8 (3 WITHOUT SOUND) 10
SOURCE OF POWER! SUPER BONEY / WIZARD WOOD
PROTECTION OF HOME AREA: 16 SPELLS

EXTRAS: "TIGER" – FULL SCALE (SIZE) DRAGON

WEAPONS CLASSIFICATIONS:
DAGGER 7   POLE ARMS 8
HAND AX 8   HALBEAR 8
MACE 6   2 HND. SWORD 3
SWORD 6   MTD. LANCE 9
BATTLE AXE 10 + 5   PIKE 7
MORN. STAR 6   AGURBOS 7
FLAIL 7   STONE 6
SPEAR 5   CROSSBOW 4
LONG BOW 6   L. CAT 10

AS YOU CAN SEE, HIS ATTRIBUTES CHANGED BASED ON LEVELING UP, WHICH WAS ANOTHER THING ARNESON EXPANDED ON.

CHARACTER ATTRIBUTES WERE FIRST DEVELOPED BY DAVE ARNESON, BUT HE WAS INSPIRED BY TONY BATH.

A GAME BATH CREATED CALLED HYBORIA USED LIMITED CHARACTER ATTRIBUTES TO GAUGE HOW NPCS RESPONDED TO DIFFERENT SITUATIONS.

THIS LED TO ARNESON ESTABLISHING A SERIES OF EXPANDED CHARACTER ATTRIBUTES IN BLACKMOOR, INCLUDING STRENGTH, BRAINS, SEX, COURAGE, CREDIBILITY, HEALTH, AND LOOKS.

MOST WOULD CARRY OVER INTO D&D, WHERE, AFTER SOME TINKERING, THEY BECAME STRENGTH, DEXTERITY, INTELLIGENCE, WISDOM, CHARISMA, AND CONSTITUTION.

CHARACTER SHEETS DIDN'T HAVE A SET FORMAT AT FIRST. EVEN WHEN IT CAME TO EARLY VERSIONS OF DUNGEONS & DRAGONS.

INSTEAD, PLAYERS WOULD SUBMIT TEMPLATES TO TTRPG ZINES, UNTIL THEY WERE EVENTUALLY RESTRICTED FROM DOING SO WHEN D&D ISSUED ITS OWN.

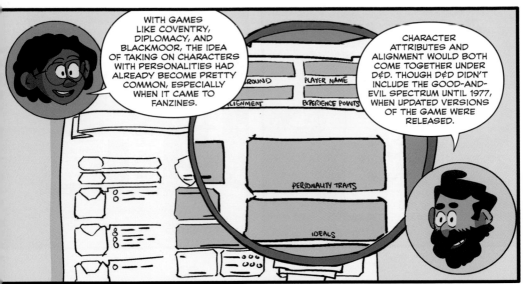

WITH GAMES LIKE COVENTRY, DIPLOMACY, AND BLACKMOOR, THE IDEA OF TAKING ON CHARACTERS WITH PERSONALITIES HAD ALREADY BECOME PRETTY COMMON, ESPECIALLY WHEN IT CAME TO FANZINES.

CHARACTER ATTRIBUTES AND ALIGNMENT WOULD BOTH COME TOGETHER UNDER D&D. THOUGH D&D DIDN'T INCLUDE THE GOOD-AND-EVIL SPECTRUM UNTIL 1977, WHEN UPDATED VERSIONS OF THE GAME WERE RELEASED.

ARRIVING AT THE MODERN CHARACTER SHEET WAS A PROCESS OF AMALGAMATION, BASED ON BORROWING AND REWORKING IDEAS FROM DIFFERENT GAME DESIGNERS OVER TIME. WHAT LED TO GAMES LIKE D&D WAS REMOVING WARFARE AS THE PRIMARY GOAL OF PLAY.

WHAT WAS FORMERLY JUST A GENERAL OR A KING OR A BARON FOR THE PURPOSES OF IDENTIFICATION ALONE WAS GIVEN A SPECIFIC BACKGROUND AND COULD GO ON ADVENTURES, EXPLORE DUNGEONS, FORGE FRIENDSHIPS, OR ACQUIRE ENEMIES.

ATTRIBUTES AND SKILLS HAVE EVOLVED OVER TIME AND ARE NOW DEPENDENT ON THE GAME IN QUESTION, BUT IN THEM RESIDES A RECORD OF THE PAST.

GYGAX AND ARNESON PUBLISHED THE FIRST EDITION OF DUNGEONS & DRAGONS IN JANUARY 1974.

AT FIRST IT SOLD MODESTLY. IT WASN'T AN INSTANT HIT.

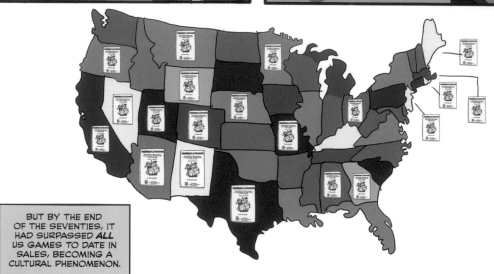

BUT BY THE END OF THE SEVENTIES, IT HAD SURPASSED *ALL* US GAMES TO DATE IN SALES, BECOMING A CULTURAL PHENOMENON.

BUT WHY DID THIS HAPPEN? WE'VE GONE THROUGH CHUNKS OF HUMAN HISTORY AS IT PERTAINS TO IMAGINATIVE PLAY.

BUT WHY DID D&D IN PARTICULAR, AND NOT OTHERS RESEMBLING IT, END UP BEING THE TECTONIC SHIFT?

THE ANSWER WILL CONTINUE TO BE DEBATED, BUT STORYTELLING, AND MYTHOLOGICAL STORYTELLING IN PARTICULAR, MAY HOLD SOME CLUES.

Part Six

CONTINUING
THE ADVENTURE

THIS CAN BE SEEN IN THE CHINESE WARRIOR TALES WE SPOKE OF EARLIER, LIKE HUANG OF THE EASTERN SEA, THE MAGICIAN WHO FIGHTS TIGERS WITH HIS GOLDEN SWORD.

A LOT OF THE FANTASY LITERATURE WE DISCUSSED STEMS FROM STORIES AND LEGENDS. FROM MAGIC SWORDS AND RINGS TO TERRIBLE MONSTERS AND THE HEROES THAT DEFEAT THEM, ALL OF THEIR ROOTS ARE IN ANCIENT MYTHOLOGY, WHERE GODS AND DEMONS FOUGHT FOR CONTROL OF THE COSMOS.

IN FACT, MYTHOLOGICAL STORIES CROSS CULTURAL LINES AND OFTEN RESEMBLE EACH OTHER, LIKE THESE TWO GODS WHOSE AXES PRODUCE THUNDER.

MAYAN DEITY

YORUBA DEITY

THOUGH JOSEPH CAMPBELL, A PROFESSOR OF LITERATURE WHO STUDIED COMPARATIVE RELIGION AND MYTHOLOGY, HAS BEEN CRITIQUED FOR OVERSIMPLIFYING NON-WESTERN CULTURES, HIS WORK ON MYTH HAS BEEN INFLUENTIAL.

HIS MONOMYTH THEORY VENTURES THAT ALL MYTHS ARE VARIATIONS ON ONE COMMON HUMAN STORY, WHICH WE SHARE IN A PSYCHIC, UNCONSCIOUS SENSE.

CALL TO ADVENTURE

SUPERNATURAL AID

RETURN

KNOWN UNKNOWN

THE HERO'S JOURNEY

THRESHOLD

ATONEMENT

CHALLENGES

TRANSFORMATION

ABYSS

PSYCHOLOGIST CARL JUNG, WHO WE MENTIONED EARLIER, SHARED CAMPBELL'S SENTIMENTS IN HIS WRITINGS ABOUT ARCHETYPES, AND MULTIPLE SCHOLARS, WRITERS, AND ARTISTS EXPLORE SUCH CONCEPTS TO THIS DAY AND EXPAND UPON THEM.

D&D USED FANTASY TO BUILD ITS WORLD, AND FANTASY DERIVES FROM MYTHS, THE OLDEST HERO STORIES ON THE PLANET. D&D ALLOWED PEOPLE TO NOT ONLY TAKE IN SUCH STORIES, BUT CRAWL INSIDE THEM.

SINCE TTRPGS ALLOW FOR DIRECT PARTICIPATION, THEY GET AT THE HEART OF WISH FULFILLMENT.

WHICH IS A BIG REASON PEOPLE READ FICTION TO BEGIN WITH.

PARTICULARLY ADVENTURE FICTION WITH HERO NARRATIVES, MAGIC TREASURES, AND DANGEROUS MONSTERS.

BUT ALL OF THAT SAID, FANTASY ONLY ACTED AS THE CONDUIT FOR THE FIRST MODERN TTRPGS.

SINCE THE MEDIUM IS CONSTANTLY EVOLVING, IT HAS BEEN MADE MORE INTERESTING BY INCLUDING OTHER GENRES.

THIS HAS ALSO INVOLVED EXPANDING BEYOND ALL-WHITE, ALL-MALE GAMING SPACES TO INCLUDE OTHER NECESSARY VOICES.

151

...TS HAVE OCCURRED AS NONWHITE, ...RANS, NONBINARY, DISABLED, ...EURODIVERSE, AND GAMERS OF ...ARGINALIZED GENDER HAVE WORKED HARDER TO INCREASE INCLUSION.

THESE EFFORTS HAVE NOT ONLY LED TO DIVERSITY AMONG PLAYERS, BUT DIVERSITY AMONG GAMES THEMSELVES. BUT THERE'S STILL A LOT OF WORK TO DO.

I'M NOT PERSONALLY A FAN OF FANTASY, BUT I LOVE SCIENCE FICTION! AND THERE ARE FAR MORE SCI-FI TTRPGS NOW TO CHOOSE FROM.

OTHER GENRES HAVE MADE THEIR WAY INTO THE FOLD AS WELL, AND THEY ARE CONSTANTLY BEING BLENDED, COMBINED, AND RECOMBINED.

FANTASY STILL REMAINS MONOLITHIC IN TERMS OF WHAT GAMERS TEND TO PLAY, BUT EXCITING NEW WORLDS ARE BEING CHARTED EVERY DAY, WHICH IS IMPORTANT TO KEEP TTRPGS EVOLVING AS GAMES HAVE THROUGHOUT TIME.

I WAS EVEN INVITED TO PLAY A WRESTLING TTRPG RECENTLY.

THE IDEA OF FANTASY NEEDS TO BE REINVENTED AS WELL. IT SHOULDN'T ALWAYS TRANSLATE TO WHITE AND WESTERN. EVERY CULTURE HAS MYTHS AND MAGIC, NOT JUST EUROPE.

THE GROUPS I PLAY TTRPGS WITH ARE DIVERSE IN BACKGROUND AND ORIENTATION.

THE EXACT SAME IS TRUE FOR ME. NOTIONS OF TTRPG SPACES BEING DOMINATED BY MIDDLE-CLASS AND UPPER-MIDDLE-CLASS WHITE PEOPLE IS OLD-FASHIONED.

ANOTHER BARRIER I ALWAYS RAN INTO WHEN PLAYING TTRPGS WAS THAT THE MYRIAD GUIDEBOOKS WERE LONG AND EXPENSIVE.

I'M ABSOLUTELY NOT READING ANY OF THESE BOOKS.

THANKFULLY, EVEN D&D AND OTHER TTRPGS HAVE BEEN ATTEMPTING TO BREAK DOWN THESE BARRIERS, PERTAINING TO BOTH COST AND TIME.

WHEW

ANOTHER THING THAT WE SHOULD ALSO REMEMBER IS THAT TTRPGS AREN'T LIMITED TO GIGANTIC CHARACTER-BASED CAMPAIGNS THAT PLAY OUT OVER A SERIES OF MONTHS OR, IN THE CASE OF SOME GAMES THAT I'VE PLAYED, YEARS.

THIS IS OUR NINE HUNDRED AND FIFTIETH SESSION. CAN YOU BELIEVE IT?

THERE ARE TTRPGS THAT CAN BE PLAYED IN ONE DAY, ONE HOUR, WITH GROUPS OF PEOPLE, OR ON YOUR OWN. TAKE THE FIGHTING FANTASY GAME BOOKS BY STEVE JACKSON AND IAN LIVINGSTONE.

THESE BOOKS, CONSIDERED CLASSICS BY SOME AND MORE POPULAR IN THE UK THAN IN THE UNITED STATES, ALLOWED FOR A GREAT DEAL OF WHAT GOES INTO TTRPGS TO BE PLAYED ON ONE'S OWN, WITH ONLY THE BOOK AND A SET OF DICE.

AND DESPITE THE TITLE OF THE SERIES, THEY AREN'T LIMITED TO THE FANTASY GENRE. IT'S GOOD TO KNOW THAT THERE ARE WAYS TO ENTER THE WORLD OF TTRPGS THAT DON'T INVOLVE A PLAYER'S HANDBOOK, DUNGEON MASTER'S GUIDE, AND CAMPAIGN MODULES.

MANUALS AREN'T BAD THINGS IN ANY WAY. I PERSONALLY LOVE DIVING INTO BIG BOOKS WHEN I FIRST GET AHOLD OF THEM TO SEARCH OUT AND UNDERSTAND RULES. BUT NOT EVERYONE HAS THAT DESIRE, TIME, OR ABILITY, AND THERE ARE PLENTY OF WONDERFUL OPTIONS.

WHEN IT COMES DOWN TO IT, ALL YOU REALLY NEED TO PLAY A TTRPG IS AN IMAGINATION, A STORY, AND SOME WAY TO SEE WHETHER YOUR ACTIONS ARE SUCCESSFUL.

THIS BRINGS ME TO ANOTHER GREAT KIND OF ROLEPLAYING.

LARPING!

PERHAPS THE MOST ACTIVE FORM OF INDIVIDUAL PARTICIPATION IN GAMING COMES IN THE FORM OF LARPING.

THIS IS WHERE THE ACTION IS.

LARPING TAKES ITS ROOTS FROM HISTORICAL REENACTMENT.

SPECIFICALLY, IT STEMS FROM **THE SOCIETY FOR CREATIVE ANACHRONISM,** FOUNDED BY DIANA PAXSON. REMEMBER—THIS GROUP WAS COVENTRY'S SPIRITUAL SUCCESSOR.

SOCIETY OF ANACHRONISM
- EST. 1966 -

PARTICIPANTS WERE ENCOURAGED TO EXHIBIT ACTIVE AGENCY AS THEY PARTICIPATED IN A FORM OF IMPROVISATIONAL THEATER...BUT ONE GOVERNED BY RULES.

WITH THE EMERGENCE OF DUNGEONS & DRAGONS IN 1974, FANTASY LARPING BEGAN SPRINGING UP AROUND THE COUNTRY. SEEMINGLY INDEPENDENT OF D&D!

AND ONE DAY, IT WOULD MAKE ITS WAY AROUND TO ME...

ST. LOUIS, MO
2008

ARA
(DORM HALL NEIGHBOR)

DO YOU GUYS WANNA PLAY DAG WITH US?

MISSY
(COLLEGE ROOMMATE)

WHAT'S DAG?

TO THE COMMON ROOM!

DAG IS SHORT FOR DAGORHIR! IT'S A TYPE OF LIVE ACTION ROLEPLAYING GAME! HERE, WATCH THIS VIDEO FROM LAST YEAR'S RAGNAROK!

WE MAKE OUR OWN WEAPONS AND COSTUMES, AND WE PICK TEAMS (OR REALMS); AND WE PLAY ALL SORTS OF LARPING GAMES!

LIKE CAPTURE THE FLAG?

SORT OF...HERE ARE ALL KINDS OF GAMES WE PLAY.

DREAM

RAGNAROK

2005

THERE'S ONE GAME WHERE THE GOAL IS TO PROTECT ONE CHARACTER, WHILE THE OTHERS HAVE TO MAKE THEIR WAY TO A GOAL WITHOUT GETTING KILLED.

2005

AND IF YOU GET HIT IN BOTH LEGS AND BOTH ARMS, YOU'RE OFFICIALLY DEAD AND HAVE TO LIE ON THE GROUND UNTIL THE ROUND IS OVER.

SO THERE ARE PLENTY OF RULES ABOUT WHAT YOU CAN AND CAN'T DO, BUT IT'S MOSTLY FUN BECAUSE OF THE COSTUMES AND WEAPONS!

I'M IN.

DAGORHIR WAS ONE OF THE BEST PARTS OF MY COLLEGE EXPERIENCE. I LOVED MAKING MY COSTUMES.

I LEARNED HOW TO MAKE WEAPONS FROM FOAM AND PVC.

THWAK!!

I ALSO LEARNED HOW TO TEST THEM TO MAKE SURE THEY WERE PROPERLY MADE AND WOULDN'T HURT ANYONE.

THIS ONE COULD USE MORE FOAM.

SOON AFTER WE STARTED, WE HEADED TO OUR FIRST TOURNAMENT IN CARBONDALE.

THERE WAS FOOD AND DANCE AND SEVERAL REALMS THAT SHOWED UP TO BATTLE!

SIGN UP HERE

The Shire of Byzantium

TRASH

TRASH

YOUR HIGHNESS.

WELCOME TO YOUR FIRST TOURNAMENT! ARA'S TOLD US YOU'VE ALL BEEN EXCITED TO JOIN US. WE WELCOME YOU WITH OPEN ARMS.

AIM AND FIRE!

HUFF! HUFF!

AT THE END OF THE TOURNAMENT (WHICH WE DEFINITELY LOST), WE ALL SAT AROUND THE BONFIRE AND TOLD STORIES OF PAST VICTORIES AND FUTURE GOALS WITHIN OUR RESPECTIVE REALMS.

THIS WAS EXACTLY WHAT I WANTED...

...MORE ROLEPLAYING THAN GAMING, AND MORE IMMERSION THAN A TALE AND MINIATURES COULD PROVIDE.

ONCE I LEFT SCHOOL, THAT WAS THE END OF MY TIME WITH LARPING. BUT I CAN STILL MAKE A MEAN SHORT SWORD.

THERE ISN'T A BIG DIFFERENCE BETWEEN YOU LARPING AND ME PLAYING TEENAGE MUTANT NINJA TURTLES IN MY FRIEND'S BACKYARD. ONE JUST HAS MORE ELABORATE COSTUMES AND A FEW STANDARDIZED RULES.

THOUGH LARPING WAS GIVEN A NAME AFTER THE RISE OF MODERN TTRPGS, THE PRACTICE GOES AS FAR BACK AS IMAGINATIVE PLAY.

BRING BACK THE SACRED GEM, THIEF!

I'D RATHER DESTROY IT THAN HAND IT OVER!

IN A WAY, ROLEPLAYING GAMES HAVE BEEN AROUND SINCE HUMAN BEINGS FIRST PLAYED PRETEND, WHICH MAY BE AS OLD AS OUR SPECIES.

INTO THE VOLCANO!

THE GEM!!

159

IT'S ALSO WORTH MENTIONING THAT TTRPGS HAVE PSYCHOLOGICAL, COMMUNAL, AND SOCIETAL BENEFITS.

EXTENSIVE STUDIES HAVE BEEN DONE INVOLVING KIDS ON THE AUTISM SPECTRUM AND THE BENEFITS OF PLAYING TTRPGS.

THERE'S AN OGRE ATTACKING!

ONE STUDY THAT EMERGED IN 2015 TRACKS A SUMMER CAMP FOR CHILDREN ON THE AUTISM SPECTRUM.

CAN I HOLD THE GATE OPEN TO HELP MY FRIENDS?

ROLL FOR STRENGTH!

THE CAMP REVOLVED AROUND COLLABORATIVE STORYTELLING, IMPROVISATIONAL THEATER, AND TTRPG GAMES LIKE D&D. THE STUDY ARGUED THAT THE KIDS WHO ATTENDED THE CAMP BENEFITTED IN MYRIAD WAYS.

THE STRUCTURED SOCIAL PRACTICE OF ROLEPLAYING GAMES, THE PERSONALIZED CHARACTER SHEETS, ALIGNMENTS, AND FANTASY-BASED HERO STORIES LED TO INCREASED SOCIAL COORDINATION.

THAT WAS A GOOD IDEA!

THANKS!

A SHARED FANTASY WORLD AND SET GUIDES FOR LAW, ORDER, GOOD, AND EVIL WERE USEFUL TO KIDS ON THE AUTISM SPECTRUM.

PLAYERS COULD CREATE CHARACTERS WITH SET TRAITS THAT BECAME SOURCES OF CONSISTENCY WHEN IT CAME TO SELF-EXPRESSION.

FOLLOWING THE CAMP, ITS ATTENDEES EXPERIENCED NOTICEABLE SOCIAL BENEFITS.

BEFORE, MANY KIDS ON THE AUTISM SPECTRUM EXPERIENCED DIFFICULTIES PLAYING D&D WITH CAMPERS NOT ON THE SPECTRUM. BY THE END OF THE PROGRAM, THEY COULD HAVE FUN ENGAGING WITH ALL GROUPS.

ROLEPLAYING GAMES WERE SHOWN TO BE TRANSFORMATIVE IN HELPING PEOPLE WITH DIFFERING COMMUNICATION STYLES TO DEVELOP AND GROW.

MANY KINDS OF PEOPLE CAN RELATE TO HAVING TRANSFORMATIVE EXPERIENCES PLAYING TTRPGS.

THIS IS ESPECIALLY TRUE WHEN IT COMES TO TAKING LESSONS LEARNED INSIDE THE GAME, OUTSIDE OF THE GAME.

TTRPG PLAYERS REGULARLY REPORT ACTUAL LIFE CHANGES DIRECTLY INFLUENCED BY THEIR ROLE-PLAYING CAMPAIGNS.

THIS COULD BE A MEEK PERSON ACTING BOLD OR SOMEONE ASSUMING THE ROLE OF A CHARACTER WITH A GENDER IDENTITY THAT FEELS MORE FITTING TO THEM.

HEY, Y'ALL! MY CHARACTER GOES BY THEY/THEM PRONOUNS.

INHABITING DIFFERENT ROLES CHALLENGES ASSUMPTIONS, AND COLLECTIVE STORYTELLING ENCOURAGES THE NAVIGATION OF COMPLEX SOCIAL ISSUES.

COOL!

GOT IT!

THIS ISN'T TO SAY THERE AREN'T ISSUES IN THE TTRPG COMMUNITY AS A WHOLE. DISCRIMINATION AND BULLYING DO OCCUR AS WELL AS APPROPRIATION AND MICROAGGRESSIONS.

BUT MANY INDIVIDUAL GROUPS WILL OFTEN MAINTAIN ORDER (AND FUN) AMONG THEMSELVES BY CREATING A UNIQUE SET OF ETHICAL RULES.

FOR ME, I'VE TAKEN MANY VALUABLE WRITING LESSONS FROM TTRPGS. NOTABLE AMONG THEM CHARACTER DEVELOPMENT AND IMPROVISATION. IN TTRPGS, PLAYERS RARELY REACT AS YOU HOPE THEY WILL. AND EVEN IF THEY DO, YOU MUST BE READY TO LET THE STORY HEAD IN UNEXPECTED DIRECTIONS.

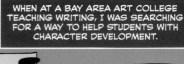

WHEN AT A BAY AREA ART COLLEGE TEACHING WRITING, I WAS SEARCHING FOR A WAY TO HELP STUDENTS WITH CHARACTER DEVELOPMENT.

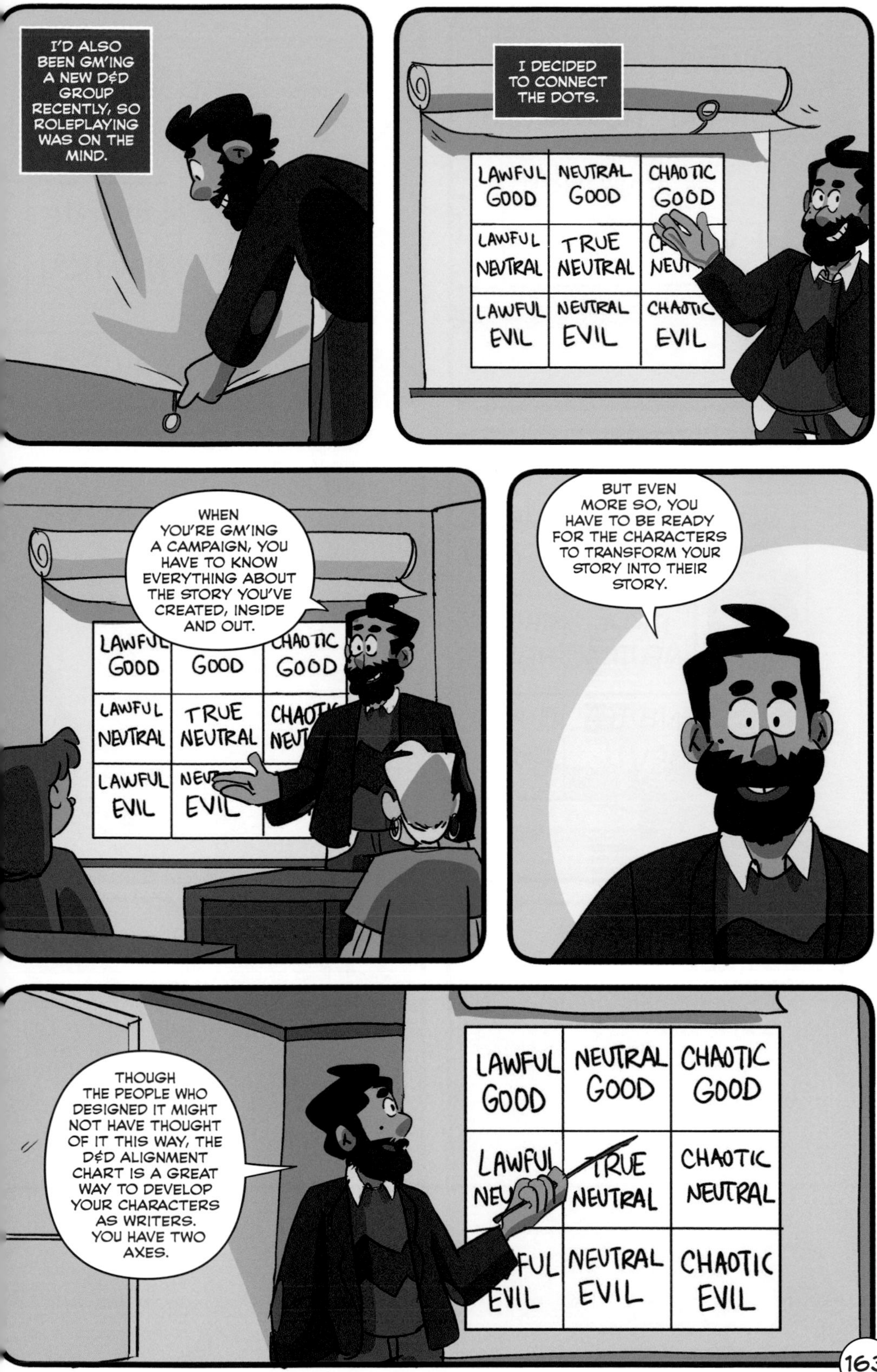

I'D ALSO BEEN GM'ING A NEW D&D GROUP RECENTLY, SO ROLEPLAYING WAS ON THE MIND.
I DECIDED TO CONNECT THE DOTS.
LAWFUL GOOD
NEUTRAL GOOD
CHAOTIC GOOD
LAWFUL NEUTRAL
TRUE NEUTRAL
LAWFUL EVIL
NEUTRAL EVIL
CHAOTIC EVIL
WHEN YOU'RE GM'ING A CAMPAIGN, YOU HAVE TO KNOW EVERYTHING ABOUT THE STORY YOU'VE CREATED, INSIDE AND OUT.
BUT EVEN MORE SO, YOU HAVE TO BE READY FOR THE CHARACTERS TO TRANSFORM YOUR STORY INTO THEIR STORY.
THOUGH THE PEOPLE WHO DESIGNED IT MIGHT NOT HAVE THOUGHT OF IT THIS WAY, THE D&D ALIGNMENT CHART IS A GREAT WAY TO DEVELOP YOUR CHARACTERS AS WRITERS. YOU HAVE TWO AXES.
LAWFUL GOOD
NEUTRAL GOOD
CHAOTIC GOOD
TRUE NEUTRAL
CHAOTIC NEUTRAL
NEUTRAL EVIL
CHAOTIC EVIL

THE AXIS THAT DESCRIBES YOUR CHARACTER'S VIEW OF CIVIL SOCIETY. LAW AND CHAOS.

AND THE AXIS THAT DESCRIBES YOUR CHARACTER'S VIEW OF MORALITY. GOOD AND EVIL.

AS AN EXERCISE, DIAGRAM SOME CHARACTERS FROM YOUR FAVORITE STORIES. SEE WHERE THEY FALL ON THE CHART.

THEN, TRY DIAGRAMMING YOUR OWN CHARACTERS. THOUGH YOU WON'T NECESSARILY LEARN EVERYTHING ABOUT YOUR CHARACTERS FROM AN ALIGNMENT CHART, IT'S A GREAT WAY TO ESTABLISH THEIR FUNDAMENTAL VIEWPOINTS.

AND IT'LL ALSO HELP YOU SEE WHAT KIND OF ROLE THEY PLAY IN YOUR STORY: HERO, ANTIHERO, VILLAIN, FORCE OF NATURE, OR SOMETHING THAT'S A BIT OF EACH.

SO IT'S KIND OF LIKE A BACKSTORY?

IN A WAY! IT HELPS ME GET THEM SITUATED IN THE STORY AND GIVES ME CLUES ABOUT HOW THEY WILL REACT AS IT PROGRESSES.

WOW, SO YOU USED THE ALIGNMENT CHART NOT ONLY TO BUILD THE CHARACTER, BUT TO BUILD THE STORY AROUND IT...VERY CREATIVE, SAM!

THANKS, STEENZ.

I GOT A LOT OUT OF PLAYING TTRPGS. AND I WAS GLAD TO BE ABLE TO HELP MY STUDENTS DO THE SAME!

DON'T JUST TAKE MY WORD FOR IT. DOZENS OF AUTHORS HAVE SPOKEN ABOUT HOW TTRPGS AIDED IN THEIR UNDERSTANDING OF STORY.

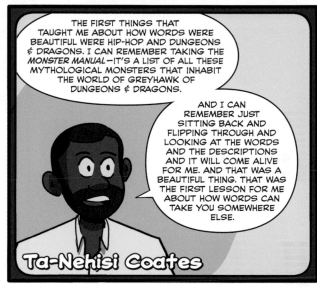

THE FIRST THINGS THAT TAUGHT ME ABOUT HOW WORDS WERE BEAUTIFUL WERE HIP-HOP AND DUNGEONS & DRAGONS. I CAN REMEMBER TAKING THE *MONSTER MANUAL*—IT'S A LIST OF ALL THESE MYTHOLOGICAL MONSTERS THAT INHABIT THE WORLD OF GREYHAWK OF DUNGEONS & DRAGONS.

AND I CAN REMEMBER JUST SITTING BACK AND FLIPPING THROUGH AND LOOKING AT THE WORDS AND THE DESCRIPTIONS AND IT WILL COME ALIVE FOR ME. AND THAT WAS A BEAUTIFUL THING. THAT WAS THE FIRST LESSON FOR ME ABOUT HOW WORDS CAN TAKE YOU SOMEWHERE ELSE.

Ta-Nehisi Coates

EVEN JUST FROM PLAYING AND DUNGEON MASTERING, I LEARNED HOW TO TELL STORIES, AND I WAS REALLY INTO THAT. YOU LEARN THINGS, ABOUT LEADERSHIP IF YOU GO TO BECOME THE PARTY LEADER, OR IF YOU'RE THE DM, YOU LEARN HOW TO KEEP PEOPLE ENGAGED, YOU LEARN HOW TO KEEP MOMENTUM, KEEP THINGS MOVING.

Gerard Way

IF DONE WELL, A GAME CAN BE A NOVEL IN ITSELF.

Sharyn McCrumb

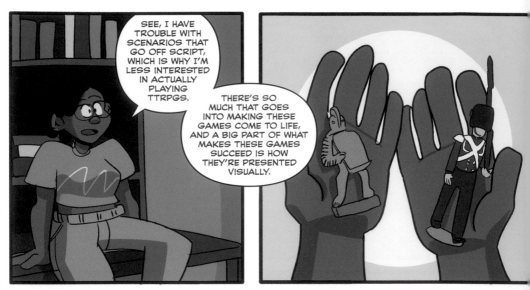

SEE, I HAVE TROUBLE WITH SCENARIOS THAT GO OFF SCRIPT, WHICH IS WHY I'M LESS INTERESTED IN ACTUALLY PLAYING TTRPGS.

THERE'S SO MUCH THAT GOES INTO MAKING THESE GAMES COME TO LIFE, AND A BIG PART OF WHAT MAKES THESE GAMES SUCCEED IS HOW THEY'RE PRESENTED VISUALLY.

GROWING UP, I KNEW A LOT OF PEOPLE WHO ONLY BOUGHT D&D BOOKS BECAUSE THEY WANTED TO LOOK AT THE ART INSIDE.

THAT, ALONGSIDE FIGURINE AND TERRAIN DESIGN, HAS BEEN A HUGE PART OF WHAT MAKES THESE GAMES INTERESTING.

THERE ARE MANY WAYS TO BECOME INVOLVED OR INTERESTED IN TTRPGS WITHOUT ACTUALLY EVEN PLAYING THEM!

YOU MIGHT JUST BE INTERESTED IN THE CULTURE THAT SURROUNDS THEM. OR YOU MIGHT ENJOY HOW THEY WORK WITH WORLDBUILDING OR ENJOY ELABORATE COSPLAY.

TTRPGS ARE ACCESSIBLE IN DIFFERENT WAYS FOR DIFFERENT PEOPLE. REGARDLESS OF YOUR INTEREST LEVEL, WHETHER YOU WANT TO PLAY OR OBSERVE, DESIGN, OR GM, THERE'S SOMETHING TO BE FOUND.

AND ISN'T THAT THE NATURE OF AN ADVENTURE? YOU, TOO, CAN BUILD UPON WHAT YOU'VE READ HERE AND INVOLVE YOURSELF IN TTRPGS IN A WAY THAT FEELS RIGHT TO YOU.

AND WHILE IT'S GREAT TO RECOGNIZE WHERE THESE GAMES CAME FROM, THEY'RE NOT ALL THAT DIFFERENT FROM PLAYING MAKE-BELIEVE IN YOUR YARD.

AN IMPORTANT PART OF WHAT WILL KEEP THE TTRPG COMMUNITY THRIVING IS MAKING SURE IT REFLECTS THE WORLD AS IT IS.

IT'S ENCOURAGING TO SEE THE WAYS IN WHICH THIS IS ALREADY OCCURRING.

Google

HOW TO RUN A TTRPG CAMPAIGN

AS BIPOC PLAYERS HAVE INCREASINGLY SEARCHED FOR REPRESENTATION IN GAMING, WE HAVE EXPANDED THE BOUNDARIES OF WHAT IT MEANS TO BE A GAMER.

SOME HAVE BEGUN AUTHORING TTRPG MATERIALS FOR LARGER COMPANIES OR CREATING GAMES ALL ON THEIR OWN.

LEARN TO DM TTRPGS 7:30PM

IT'S IMPORTANT TO UNDERSTAND THAT BREAKING DOWN BARRIERS IN GAMING COMES NOT JUST THROUGH AN INCREASED DIVERSITY OF PLAYERS. THE DIVERSITY IS ALREADY THERE. IT'S JUST NOT REPRESENTED IN MEDIA

WHAT'S NEEDED IS REPRESENTATION BEHIND THE SCENES AS WELL, WHEN IT COMES TO GAME CREATION.

AND SOME GAMERS HAVE BEGUN USING CONSENT FORMS, MAKING SURE THAT PLAYERS ARE COMFORTABLE WITH ASPECTS OF SEXUALITY AND VIOLENCE THAT MAY OCCUR WITHIN A GAME.

THINGS ARE IMPROVING, BUT WE STILL HAVE WORK TO DO SO THE GAMES WE PLAY CONTINUE TO REFLECT THE WORLD AROUND US.

KACHUNK!

ZREE!

TACK!

BAM BAM!

IT'S BEAUTIFUL.

169

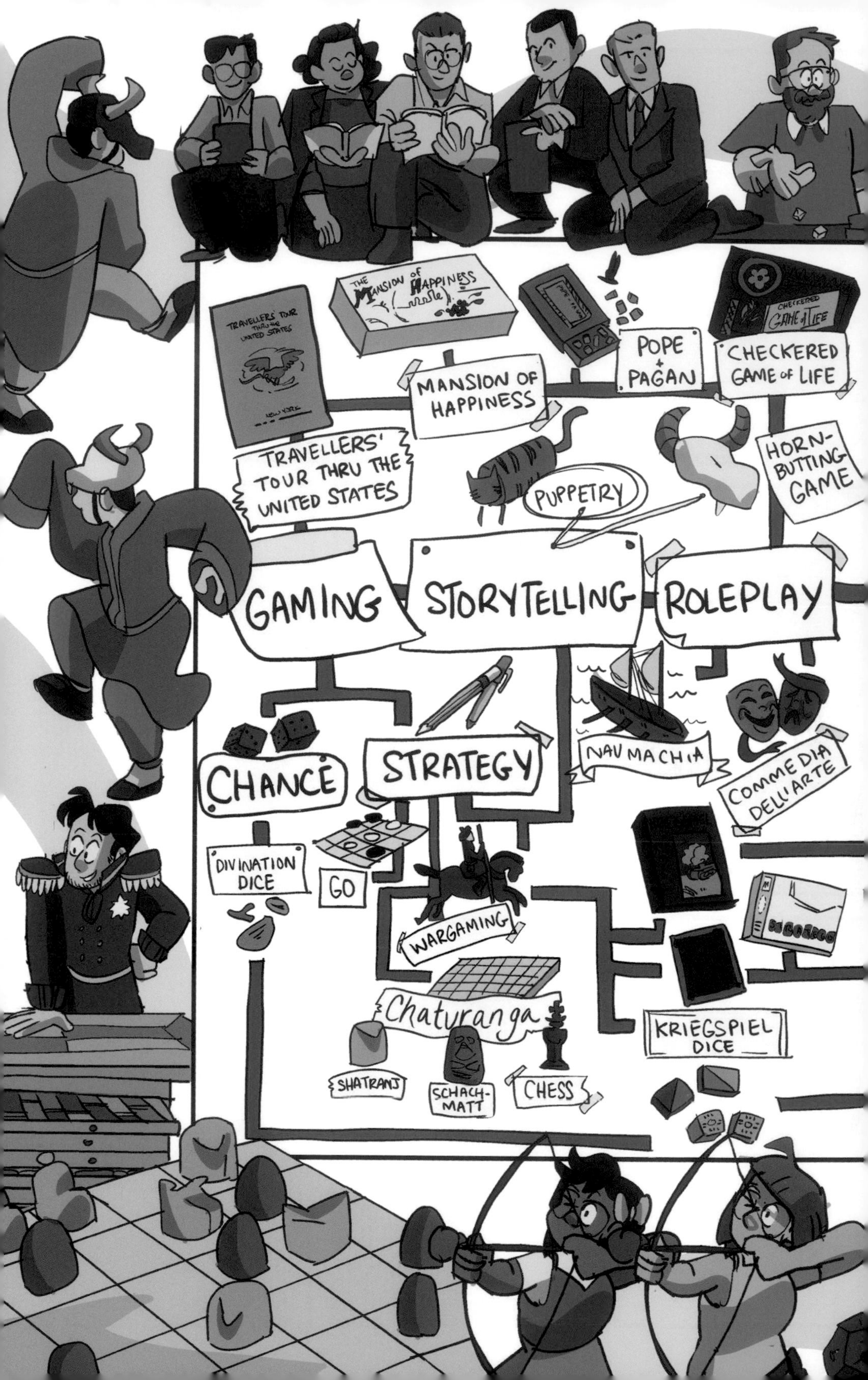

THE MANSION OF HAPPINESS
TRAVELLERS' TOUR THRU the UNITED STATES
NEW YORK
CHECKERED GAME of LIFE
POPE + PAGAN
CHECKERED GAME of LIFE
MANSION OF HAPPINESS
TRAVELLERS' TOUR THRU THE UNITED STATES
HORN-BUTTING GAME
PUPPETRY
GAMING
STORYTELLING
ROLEPLAY
CHANCE
STRATEGY
NAUMACHIA
COMMEDIA DELL'ARTE
DIVINATION DICE
GO
WARGAMING
Chaturanga
KRIEGSPIEL DICE
SHATRANJ
SCHACH-MATT
CHESS

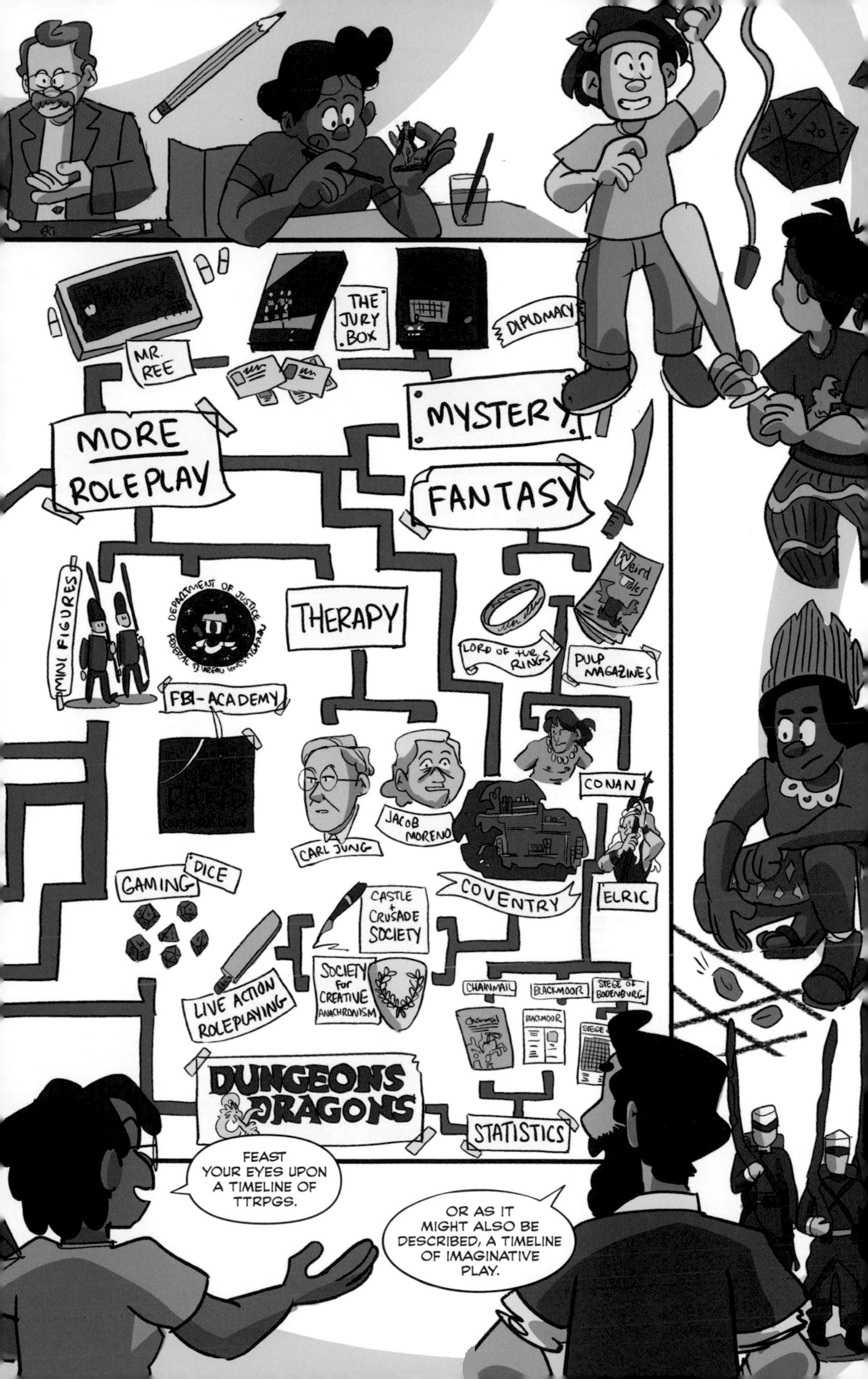
THE JURY BOX
DIPLOMACY
MR. REE
MYSTERY
MORE ROLEPLAY
FANTASY
MINI FIGURES
DEPARTMENT OF JUSTICE FEDERAL BUREAU INVESTIGATION
FBI-ACADEMY
THERAPY
Weird Tales
LORD OF THE RINGS
PULP MAGAZINES
CONAN
CARL JUNG
JACOB MORENO
GAMING
DICE
COVENTRY
ELRIC
CASTLE & CRUSADE SOCIETY
SOCIETY for CREATIVE ANACHRONISM
LIVE ACTION ROLEPLAYING
CHAINMAIL
BLACKMOOR
SIEGE OF BODENBURG
DUNGEONS & DRAGONS
STATISTICS
FEAST YOUR EYES UPON A TIMELINE OF TTRPGS.
OR AS IT MIGHT ALSO BE DESCRIBED, A TIMELINE OF IMAGINATIVE PLAY.

SO THERE YOU HAVE IT. OUR GUIDE TO TABLETOP ROLEPLAYING GAMES.

WOW. WE'RE REALLY AT THE END, *HUH*?

YES AND NO. THIS IS A SIDE QUEST. THIS ISN'T THE BE-ALL AND END-ALL OF TTRPGS. THERE'S SO MUCH MORE TO DISCOVER IF YOU HAVE THE DESIRE.

TRUE! MAYBE YOU WANT TO DIVE INTO MORE HISTORY BOOKS OR RESEARCH THE HISTORY OF ANCIENT GAMES. OR MAYBE YOU JUST WANT TO TRY AND PLAY ONE ON YOUR *OWN!*

AMASSING RULE BOOKS AND STICKING FIRMLY TO THE RULES IS ONE WAY TO PLAY THESE GAMES. BUT REALLY, EVERY TTRPG IS DIFFERENT. SOME EXIST FOR THOSE WHO WANT TO SPEND TIME BOGGED DOWN IN STATS, AND OTHERS LEAN MORE INTO COMMUNAL STORYTELLING.

WHAT'S MOST IMPORTANT IS THAT YOU TRY AND EXPLORE WHAT IT'S LIKE TO STEP OUTSIDE OF YOUR EXPERIENCE.

TO TRY, RESPONSIBLY, TO INHABIT SOMEONE ELSE'S SHOES.

ALL YOU REALLY NEED IS YOUR IMAGINATION.

STORYTELLING IS ONE OF THE FUNDAMENTAL PARTS OF WHAT MAKES US HUMAN.

SINCE TIME IMMEMORIAL, STORIES HAVE HELPED US UNDERSTAND WHAT WE ARE.

AND AS TIME GOES BY, GAMES WILL EVOLVE WITH US.

BUT THEY'LL ALWAYS BE MORE THAN JUST A GAME.

AND AS LIFE BECOMES MORE COMPLEX, SO WILL OUR GAMES.

SO WHAT DO YOU THINK?

ARE YOU READY TO PLAY?

ACKNOWLEDGMENTS

Big thanks to every friend I've ever roleplayed with. Every moment was wonderful, even when we were waiting for our turn. Thank you to my agent, Anjali Singh, for always having my back and reminding me that I do, indeed, know what I'm doing. Thank you, Aishwarya Tandon, for our late night/early morning coloring conversations. I think we learned a lot from each other. Thank you, Amanda Meadows, for the advice and encouragement throughout the drawing process. And thank you, Keya, for reminding me to eat when I was deep in drawing mode. Making a graphic novel takes a village, and I'm happy that my village is so well-rounded, knowledgeable, and sincere.

—STEENZ

Side Quest wouldn't have become the book it did without Jon Peterson and his book *Playing at the World*. Though my research was expansive, Peterson's book became the be-all and end-all for the history of modern TTRPGs, step-by-painstaking-step. I would also like to send a big shout-out to my amazing agent, Dara Hyde, who is a dungeon master of her own accord (if, by dungeon, I mean literary agency). Lastly, I'd like to thank all those kids and adults who made roleplaying games more accessible for modern generations, so that everyone, everywhere can embark on journeys of excitement and discovery.

—SAMUEL

MAGRAK'S PYLON
(A PLAYABLE ADVENTURE!)

A DUNGEONS AND DRAGONS 5TH
EDITION ADVENTURE FOR LEVEL
3: YOU WILL NEED A COPY OF THE
D&D 5E CORE RULEBOOKS TO
FULLY UTILIZE THIS ADVENTURE.

Glossary:
PC: PLAYABLE CHARACTERS
GM: GAME MASTER
DC: DIFFICULTY CLASS
HP: HIT POINTS
NPC: NONPLAYER CHARACTER

ADVENTURE SCALING: Though this
adventure is intended for Level 3 characters,
for weaker or stronger characters you
can scale the combat difficulty lower or
higher. For a stronger party, increase the
number of creature foes and raise the DC
thresholds. For a weaker party, reduce
creature encounters and DC thresholds.

PLOT: The party is concealing themselves
in a convoy bound for Magrak's Pylon,
with the intention of stealing a powerful
artifact—known as the Draga Amulet—
from a vault. Using the resources of a local
group of rebels, one of whom is wanted
by the oligarchs of Lumina City, the party
sets out and must make careful choices to
accomplish the mission and escape with the
Amulet through a teleportation tunnel.

RULES
Before you begin, ensure that you are
familiar with how the characters will fare
on an above-ground transport that is flying
more than 800 feet above the street level.
    Familiarize yourself with the rules
for espionage, sneaking, and heist.

ADVENTURE BACKGROUND
Lumina City used to be the seat of the
Rivulean Council, and thus the most
important diplomatic hub in the entire
Rivulean Galaxy. But recent crackdowns

in old leadership by the new regime have
followed the establishment of Magrak's
regime, leading to turbulence that has
echoed through not just the world of
Avarai (where this adventure takes
place), but other planets that relied on the
Council for stability. Iscaria Magrak, who
resides in a pylon in the center of Lumina
City, is a Grimonian elite who assumed
control after a propaganda campaign
aimed at scapegoating local rebels.
    Upon assuming control over Lumina
City's parliament, the Magrak engaged in
social engineering so that all of Lumina
City was embattled in constant warfare.
Through a combination of antagonizing
rebel militias and installing Iguadar
factions in the capital barracks, local
citizenry became easily cowed into
submission. Becoming a dissident now
carried a threat of death. In many ways, the
once freethinking Lumina City has begun
to take on the qualities of a police state.
    In this climate of suppression, a resistance
group led by a mercenary named Kleb
Fonarius has been creating a whisper
network throughout Lumina City. The
dissidents have been working on a way to
get ahold of a powerful artifact, the Draga
Amulet, which Magrak has used to control
the actions of Dragovores—giant beasts
that were thought to be beyond control but
which Magrak has employed in his crackdown.
    With rumors of Magrak preparing to
launch a full-blown attack on the Rivulean
Council with the help of Dragovores, swift
action is required to put a stop to it. Now,
with the PCs assembled as a mercenary group
in league with Kleb Fonarius, they will have
the chance to steal Magrak's artifact and
hobble the regime before they can lash out.

STARTING THE ADVENTURE
After searching for jobs with an
underground agency for people in need of
off-the-books work, the characters were

placed together based on their various skill sets and their willingness to work in Lumina City's seedier underground.

GM: *Welcome to the Burnlow District, where most words of import are exchanged in the shadows.*

The adventure begins in a bar called the Clunker. It isn't as loud and raucous as one might expect from a bar with such a name. Various figures huddle around tables that seem to have been assembled from spare ship parts. Whispers abound.

None of the Clunker's patrons are hostile toward the characters upon entry.

A young nonbinary person emerges from behind the bar: Kleb Fonarius. They come to the PC's table, pull up a chair. The bartender and owner, Bog, a male orc with cyborg implants covering half his face in metal, approaches with shots of a dark, rusty liquor for each character. Each PC that takes the shot will earn Kleb's trust, while any who refuse will lose that benefit for

the rest of the quest, making Kleb less likely to support them in battle.

GM: *In whispers, Kleb addresses all of you, "Though we're in the Burnlow District, our voices stay quiet. You never know how far Magrak's ear reaches . . ." They look around furtively at each of you. "My name is Kleb Fonarius, and I am in command of the Cause. But that is of no matter. What is important is that you know we must move quickly, and decisively, for our window to hobble Magrak's onslaught is narrower than it's ever been."*

Kleb then continues to explain the details of the operation. The group will disguise themselves as an automated delivery convoy bound for Magrak's Pylon, carrying luxury goods for an upcoming feast event there. The party will be concealed inside a cargo crate.

The goal of the operation is to deliver the convoy to a dock at Magrak's Pylon, unload the cargo crate, and then emerge from it. They will then crack a nearby safe barrier to gain access to the Draga Amulet and leave via a teleportation tunnel.

JETTY'S ARMS AND STORAGE

GM: *You emerge onto the streets of the Burnlow District and are entreated to the beginnings of its most notable feature: the Night Market. Stalls selling food of all kinds line the streets alongside merchant tents and tables. Kleb seems not to be interested in any of it, however, putting a hood over their head and making a beeline for a shop around the corner from the Clunker. Above the shop in blazing pink neon reads "Jetty's Arms and Storage" beside a logo of a sword-gun in profile.*

At this point, the party is encouraged to follow Kleb. If they try to stay, their point of contact will become frustrated and demand they stop doddering. As far as Kleb is concerned, the characters are on the clock and can go to the Night Market after they rendezvous at Jetty's Arms and Storage.

When they enter the shop, Kleb announces their presence to the shop owner, a thick, muscled woman named Jetty. Jetty and Kleb are friends, and Jetty expresses how happy she is that Kleb is still alive and not being torn to

pieces in an Iguadar den. Kleb informs the characters that they and Jetty go way back, but that they can't be seen together often, lest Jetty be targeted by Magrak's militias for sedition.

The reason Kleb took the characters to Jetty's is to acquire a Barrier Splitter—a device that can disable the high-potency barrier in Magrak's Pylon that guards the Draga Amulet. Barrier Splitters are illegal in Lumina City, which is why Jetty doesn't keep it on display; she takes the characters into the basement of the shop (accessed via a digitally generated hidden doorway). In the basement on a shelf is the Barrier Splitter. There are also other rare items on display, but Jetty won't be willing to sell them. If one of the characters tries to steal an item, a security system will kick in, firing rays that immobilize the thief and then sap them of all of their abilities for a full day, alongside giving them -2 on all Attack and Saving Throw rolls.

In the actual shop itself, the characters can purchase basic items and some rarer items, including the following:

- THE BADGERER: A magic ring that allows a character once per day to turn into a giant badger for four turns of combat. 75gp

- SINEWSTEALTH GLOVES: A pair of gloves that once per day can stretch a maximum of 30 feet beyond the character's normal reach (still abides by standard checks). 55gp

- SILVERTONGUE: A cyber-implant that allows the user to detect lies in perpetuity with a DC10 check. Also allows a character to perform a s uccessful lie once per day with no DC check. 128gp

After procuring the Barrier Splitter, Kleb tells the characters that they have a room reserved for them in the Clunker. Kleb will come for them at dawn to gather them for the convoy. Kleb also warns to keep their wits about them, especially if they go out and explore the Night Market.

The room provided for the characters in the rear of the Clunker is bare bones and windowless, with a simple cot for each PC to sleep on. The Clunker does not typically rent rooms, so the characters are being kept there in secret. Bog informs them that if they are to come and go then they must use the kitchen exit that leads to the back alley.

If the characters decide to go to sleep and wait for the next morning's events, the next portion does not apply.

THE NIGHT MARKET (OPTIONAL)

GM: *You emerge into the still thriving Night Market. Your senses are assailed by a mixture of food smells and your ears take in various languages—some of which you don't think you've ever heard before. You get the immediate impression that the Night Market holds endless secrets and is a place where the rarest, and most dangerous, of items could be bought, sold, and bartered, should you know where to look for them.*

When the characters enter the Night Market, they can shop for food if they'd like, trying local delicacies at 1 or 2 SP per order. Items can include things like fried eel, blood porridge, grilled demon stag, nightfish (which are large boiled worms), roasted turmeric potatoes with rosemary, and hesh eel ink soup. The characters can also go off in search of rarer finds. Most of the shopkeepers will not want to interact with the characters, given that a lot of what they're selling is contraband and requires moving off the street and behind curtained doors. Some of the items the players can discover are as follows:

- A weapons vendor named Igor sells, in addition to standard items, a magical depressurizing lance that gains a +1 bonus to attack and damage rolls made with this weapon (which deals 3d6 piercing damage against flying creatures). 165gp

- Seto, a seller of fine gloves, has sharp-fingered, jewel-studded gloves that detect magical items and enchantments,

glowing when within a 12-foot radius of anything of the sort. 48gp

- An alchemist named Baggle sells Face Gloms—devices that allow the wearer to disguise their face for 1 full day. 42gp

When the characters make their way back from the Night Market and try to enter the Clunker through the back alley doorway, they come upon a group of thieves. There are five of them (but this number can be cut down depending on the size of the party; if there are four PCs, five thieves is okay; if there are three PCs cut the number down to four; if there are two PCs cut the number down to 3; etc.):

- Barl (dwarf)

- Iko (dwarf)

- Slop (human)

- Pogo (dwarf)

- Fervus (tiefling)

The crew, led by Barl, has been following the characters since they emerged into the Night Market. They know that they're new to the Burnlow District and see them as easy prey.

They're a skilled crew, able to diffuse magical effects and rely on combat to secure what they want. They have a device called an Obviator—a small, bright purple, sea-urchin-resembling device that floats in midair above Barl. It's very hard to catch and will deactivate if Barl is killed. The Obviator nulls all magic and enchantments within a 30-foot radius. The thief crew relies upon traditional weapons for this reason.

If the characters defeat Barl first and deactivate the Obviator, the rest of his crew will flee. If they don't, the battle will take longer, and they can retrieve spoils from the deceased.

THE CONVOY

GM: *Due to the lack of windows, you don't have any idea what time it is. But when Kleb knocks loudly on the door to your room and walks in* right afterwards, you get the idea that morning has arrived. "Put some food in your bellies and then we embark. We don't have much time." Bog, the Clunker owner, brings in a tray topped with an array of mugs filled with warm broth, bread, and fruit—all in all, not a bad spread. Kleb looks over all of you and gives a decisive nod. "Meet me at the back-alley door in twenty-five minutes, and don't forget anything you won't want to have with you if we find ourselves pinned down by Iguadars...or worse."

Following Kleb's exit, breakfast, and any swift preparation, the characters should make their way to the back alley door. Kleb will be waiting with a Ground Glider—a hovering covered vehicle made for swift transport through the streets of Lumina City. The Ground Glider is bare bones on the inside, and the driver is a man named Kili wearing a cybernetic augment—a silver face shield that only reveals his eyes. If the characters wish to, they can talk to Kleb about their reasons for leading the Cause, including the rise of Magrak's militia and the crackdown on civil freedoms.

GM: *Your Ground Glider enters a warehouse district, much of which is broken down and abandoned. The streets are filled with a thick mist from a nearby water treatment plant, and you disappear into it, unable to see anything other than milky gray out the window. Moments later, you find yourself passing under a garage door, which rattles shut behind you. As you exit the Ground Glider, lights blare on, illuminating a vast warehouse with an aboveground transport stationed in its center.*

This transport is automated and doesn't require a driver. It will be transporting a load of luxury goods for Magrak's Pylon, all of which are in crates, including luxury silk robes, platinum banquet platters, holographic entertainment, and gold sculptures fashioned in Magrak's image. In the channels that aboveground transports fly, there are various security apparatuses present. The convoy itself has defense systems built in as well.

Kleb explains to the characters that they will be hiding inside one of the cargo boxes, in a hidden compartment under the cover of luxury silk robes (with scan-proof nanofibers, so they won't be detected upon entry into the Pylon). In the case that anyone boards the transport and the characters risk being discovered, they must figure out how to take out any opposition quietly or avoid detection completely.

GM: *You all crowd into the secret compartment in the back of the center of the crate along with Kleb. "There are no guarantees this will work. But if it does, we alter the future of Lumina City for the good of its people and expel Magrak and his warlords from their seat of power." You hear the rumbling of vents beneath you, and feel a pull in your stomach as you leave the ground, exit the warehouse, and glide toward the merchant delivery route above the city.*

The convoy is scanned upon entry to the merchant delivery route, and Kleb crosses their fingers. The PCs have a camera view mounted on the bough of the convoy to keep track of all activity and scan for threats.

Halfway through the voyage to Magrak's Pylon, the convoy comes to a halt. A group of Iguadar customs inspectors climbs aboard the transport, after flagging it for a reason the characters do not know. Kleb speculates it's because of the nature of the goods they're carrying.

When the Iguadars board the transport, they begin opening the crates for inspection. One Iguadar opens the container the PCs are hidden in and begins to search, coming close to discovering the hidden door. The PCs have multiple choices here. If they choose to be quiet and try to remain undetected, they each have to pass a DC13 Constitution check. The PCs can also use spells to throw off the Iguadar. Another option is to try and take the Iguadar out physically without causing a stir. Since there is a large group of them, they won't notice if one of their own is gone.

The characters can reveal themselves and start attacking the inspection crew. But if this occurs, the pilot will lose control of the ship. The characters will have to regain control of the ship before it crashes into Magrak's Pylon—in which case, the mission is failed. They will also have to tussle with eleven Iguadars and, when an alert is sent out that Kleb is on the convoy, Magrak will summon a Dragovore to attack.

MAGRAK'S PYLON - THE DOCKS

The convoy approaches Magrak's Pylon. Cannons twist on swivels to follow its trajectory as you descend to ground level and into the unloading dock. A group of Igaudars with legers clicks notes into tablets as they account for each item, and a transport begins to lift the crates off the convoy one by one. Soon enough, your crate is being lifted—you're not sure to where. Eventually, after a few uneasy moments, you're deposited on the ground, and sit in silence for a bit, listening for movement. Hearing nothing in the immediate vicinity, Kleb decides to shuffle the hidden compartment door aside and investigate.

Kleb tells the characters they can emerge, but urges caution. The crate the characters came in was placed on the ground in a storage area. But a successful Intelligence/Perception DC11 check will alert the characters to a nearby group of Iguadars having a coffee break. The Iguadars are as follows:

- Slack

- Morphan

- Doolis

If the characters continue to observe, they'll overhear that this trio is in the very lucrative business of skimming goods from the delivery convoys for their own designs. Slack and Doolis start talking about the luxury shipment that just came in for a banquet at the Pylon in Magrak's honor and decide they should take advantage of their fortune. After looking around for other Iguadars, the three approach the cargo the characters came in, and the PCs must decide what to do. One thing they don't want to happen is to set off the alarm. If in any case, one of the Iguadars makes it to a button on the wall on the opposite side of

the dock, the alarm will sound and twelve more Iguadars will pile in for a fight. If this happens, it doesn't result in the adventure's failure, but it will add more danger to using the Barrier Splitter to recover the Amulet.

If the dozen Iguadars attack, the characters can fight or try to hide in the air ducts, which Klebs knows the route to. They can also try and distract or confuse the Iguadars.

THE ARTIFACT

GM: *Kleb leads you down a corridor, and then hops into a vent, beckoning the rest of you to follow. They've obviously mapped every inch of this compound, studied it extensively. As you follow Kleb through the vents, you wonder if you can be heard below, but before you have too much time to contemplate, Kleb opens a vent. They toss down two pellets through a hatch, and you hear a slight hissing sound, followed by two heavy thumps. Kleb propels themselves downward and when you all assemble beside them, you see two felled guards in front of a large glowing barrier, beyond which lies the Draga Amulet.*

The barrier itself must be broken with the Barrier Splitter. But the process takes a while, and in the time the characters are standing by an encounter will occur. Use the d20 as follows to decide the encounter:

1–5: Another two Iguadar guards come by to relieve the unconscious ones present at the entrance to the barrier. They will attack immediately on sight and try to radio for backup. Calling for backup would lead to a dozen Iguadars showing up to attack. (If the dozen Iguadars have already been dealt with, call in six more.)

6–10: An automated defense drone on patrol will happen upon the characters and attack.

11–19: One of Magrak's mages visiting the Draga Amulet chamber to activate the artifact comes upon the characters.

This character, a human man named Ulstar Frak, is a level 6 sorcerer and has a magical weapon (detailed in stat block).

20: One of the guards awakes and alerts the others—the party is attacked by a dozen Iguadars as they try to split the barrier. (If the dozen Iguadars have already been dealt with, call in six more, along with an automated defense drone.)

GM: *It comes as no small relief when the Barrier Splitter teems with energy, glows bright yellow, and issues a high-powered laser. In one swift downward arc, that laser severs the barrier right down the middle. Now, the Amulet chamber is in full view. It's a simple room, protected by who-knows-how-many reinforced steel walls, in the middle of which sits a small marble podium. Upon that podium is the Draga Amulet, a silver, Dragovore shaped pendant with a yellow stone at its center.*

One of the characters must choose to take the Amulet; Kleb will be reluctant, due to a need to maintain the focus to get them to the teleportation tunnel. Whichever character grabs it will notice it starts to glow white hot. The PCs then hear an ear-shattering roar as a Dragovore crashes through the wall. At this point, if the rest of the Iguadars haven't been alerted yet, they are now, and come running into the room to find a giant Dragovore staring them down (if the Iguadar squad has already been dealt with, another group will show up, fifteen strong). The character wielding the Amulet can now control the Dragovore. But keep in mind that doing this is no simple task. Every single action the character wishes to ask of the Dragovore requires a DC15. If the character fails, then the Dragovore loses focus and spins out of control, dealing 1d8 damage to each PC within a forty-foot vicinity. Even if the PC with the Amulet issues no commands, however, since they hold the Amulet, the Dragovore will attack the Iguadars.

Three combat turns must pass while Kleb sets up a teleportation tunnel. They use what's called a Portal Spinner to do so. It's a device that's placed on the ground and then begins spinning at hypersonic speeds to generate a tunnel.

ENDING THE ADVENTURE

When the characters step into the teleportation tunnel, they are transported to a rooftop outside of Magrak's Pylon. The Dragovore bursts from the inside of the Pylon, leaving a gigantic hole in it. Kleb then asks the character holding the Amulet to place it inside a protective chamber, isolating it so that the characters won't attract the Dragovore. If the PC refuses, the Dragovore continues to cause havoc around the city and the adventure fails.

GM: *After you place the Draga Amulet in Kleb's containment device, you notice a palpable calm take hold, along with a sense of triumph as the flames grow and grow from Magrak's Pylon. Kleb smiles at you. "This is the beginning of the end for Magrak. Thanks to all of you, Lumina City may yet shine again."*

Back at the Cause headquarters, the characters are honored as heroes and receive official guild membership. Kleb informs the player who used the Amulet that the possibility has been raised that, for the rest of their life, they will have a connection to Dragovores and will be able to communicate with (but not control) them.

The characters leave the Cause headquarters and emerge back into the Burnlow District. It's a new day in Lumina City. But the work is just beginning.

REWARDS

Players earn 1500xp for recovering the Amulet and entering the teleportation tunnel. Since it is up to the players as to which creature encounters take place, creature XP should be added as needed based on encounters.

STAT BLOCKS

We have provided a couple of sample stat blocks for NPC encounters.
You may improvise as necessary for other encounters.

IGUADARS

ARMOR CLASS 12 (light bio-armor, shield)
HIT POINTS 12 (2d8+3)
SPEED 25 ft. swim 30 ft

STR	DEX	CON	INT	WIS	CHA
12 (+1)	12 (+1)	13 (+1)	10 (+0)	10 (+0)	7 (-1)

SAVING THROWS Str +1, Dex +5, Con +2

SKILLS Stealth +4

SENSES passive Perception 11

LANGUAGES Iguadar and Common

CHALLENGE ¼ (100 XP)

LAND AND WATER
The Iguadars can breathe underwater
and above ground.

CAMOUFLAGE
When attempting to attack
undetected, Iguadars can blend
in with their surroundings,
giving them advantage on
Dexterity (Stealth) checks.

ACTIONS

MULTIATTACK
The Iguadar can make two melee
attacks or three ranged attacks.

LASER LASSO
Reach 11 ft. and range
30/70 ft., one target.
Hit: 11 (2d4 + 2) shock damage.
Can induce hold for one turn,
requiring a character to make
a DC strength to escape.

DRAGAVORE

ARMOR CLASS 21 (natural armor)
HIT POINTS 400 (22d20 + 160)
SPEED 40 ft., fly 80 ft., swim 40 ft.

STR	DEX	CON	INT	WIS	CHA
27 (+8)	12 (+1)	25 (+7)	20 (+5)	17 (+3)	19 (+4)

SAVING THROWS Dex +8, Con +14, Wis +10, Cha +11

SKILLS Deception +15, Insight +7, Perception +20, Persuasion +14, Stealth +10

DAMAGE IMMUNITIES poison, fire

SENSES blindsight 100 ft., darkvision 140 ft., passive Perception 32

LANGUAGES Common, Psychic, Dragovore

CHALLENGE 20 (37000 XP)

THE AMULET'S HOLD
Magrak can use the Draga Amulet to exercise control over the Dragavore, overriding its instincts to proceed according to his will.

ACTIONS

FIRE BREATH
The dragon exhales flames in a 120-foot radius. All creatures in the zone of contact must make a DC 22 Constitution saving throw, taking 68 (12d8) fire damage on a failed save, and a third of that if the save is successful.

CHOMP
Melee Weapon Attack: +14 to hit, reach 20 ft., one target.
Hit: 16 (2d8 + 8) piercing damage.

CLAWS
Melee Weapon Attack: +14 to hit, reach 8 ft., one target.
Hit: 20 (3d8 + 8) slashing damage.

TAIL SWIPE
Melee Weapon Attack: +12 to hit, reach 30 ft., one target.
Hit: 14 (2d6 + 8) bludgeoning damage.

GLOSSARY

ALIGNMENT: The way in which a player's moral and ethical perspective is classified in many major TTRPGs, involving a strata of good, neutral, and evil on the moral side, and lawful, neutral, and chaotic on the ethics side.

ARMOR CLASS: The way in which a character or monster's ability to avoid being hit during combat is determined.

BAIXI (HUNDRED ENTERTAINMENTS): Established during the Han Dynasty, an ancient circus featuring variety shows, jugglers, theater acrobats, magicians, dancers, and more.

THE BLACKMOOR CAMPAIGN: Created by Dave Arneson in the early 1970s, the Blackmoor campaign borrowed world-building elements from The Lord of the Rings and the gothic soap opera *Dark Shadows*. Applying some of the rules from the Chainmail game, Blackmoor encouraged collaborative play in order to overcome and engage with campaign events.

THE BLACKMOOR GAZETTE AND RUMORMONGER: A campaign newsletter to accompany the Blackmoor campaign, which described various characters and exploits throughout the land, prompting more complex worldbuilding and gameplay.

CAMPAIGN: A narrative consisting of encounters, actions, Nonplayer Characters (NPCs), creatures, and more, that Player Characters can navigate under the auspices of a Game Master. A Homebrew Campaign is a term for a campaign that was created by someone unaffiliated with a games publisher.

CARL JUNG: Known as the founder of analytical psychology, Jung (1875–1961), from Switzerland, created what are known as Archetypes—universal symbols and behavioral expressions that derive from the collective unconscious.

THE CASTLE AND CRUSADE SOCIETY: A Wargames group founded by Gary Gygax and Rob Kuntz in 1970 that focused on medieval warfare. This group led to the formation of Jeff Perren's Chainmail, which fed directly into the creation of Dungeons & Dragons.

CHAINMAIL: Created by Jeff Perren in 1971, and later expanded upon by Gary Gygax, Chainmail is known as the precursor to Dungeons & Dragons. The rules were initially published in the Castle and Crusade Society's *Domesday Book* as LGTSA Miniatures Rules and would eventually introduce a 1:1 figure scale combat device. Guidon Games released its version in 1971 with a 14-page fantasy supplement that referenced various popular fantasy writers and offered combat scenarios based on specific narratives.

CHARACTER SHEET: A sheet of paper containing information for a Player Character, including statistics, alignment, background, abilities, items, and even illustrations of the character to portray their likeness. Players bring their character sheets to gaming sessions in order to keep track of what they are able to do within the confines of the game and refer to modifiers to their statistics.

CHARLES ADIEL LEWIS TOTTEN: An American military officer, professor, and writer who created Stratego: The American War Game in 1880.

CHATURANGA: The ancient Indian precursor to Chess, Chaturanga is a two-player game featuring the following pieces: Raja (King), Mantri (Counselor), Gaja (Elephant), Ashva (Knight), Bhata (Infantry), and Ratha (Chariot). The four-player variant of this game is known as Chaturaji. Shatraj is the Persian variant of Chaturanga, played in the Sasanian Empire.

THE CHECKERED GAME OF LIFE:
An early inspiration for the game Monopoly published in 1860, this game reinforced the notion that success derives from being a good disciple of Christ and will lead to both earning money and acquiring assets.

CLASS: A classification that defines a campaign member's skill set in TTRPGs. Classes may include wizard, fighter, thief, bard, ranger, and more.

COMMEDIA DELL'ARTE: Originating in sixteenth-century Italy, an interactive theater that relied on audience participation that became popular throughout Europe.

COVENTRY: Coventry was a kingdom-centered roleplaying game created in the 1950s based on the fantasy world of a man named Paul Stanbery.

DAVE ARNESON: A famed game designer who drummed up popular mechanics for modern TTRPGs and cocreated Dungeons & Dragons with Gary Gygax.

DICE: Polyhedral blocks marked with numbers or symbols, used to determine chance and outcomes in tabletop gaming.

DIPLOMACY: Created by Allan B. Calhamer in 1954 and released in 1959, Diplomacy did not use dice and was the first commercial game played by mail. Players created elaborate personas and attempted to conduct faux-statecraft over a variety of real and imagined polities.

DOMESDAY BOOK: First published by the Castle and Crusade Society, the *Domesday Book*—consisting of multiple issues—laid out rules and standards for Chainmail, the predecessor of Dungeons & Dragons. The newsletter contained various rules, maps, and gaming chapter news, and also contained early details of Dave Arneson's first fantasy roleplaying campaign, Blackmoor.

DUNGEONS & DRAGONS:
Published in 1974, the first modern tabletop roleplaying game, created by Dave Arneson and Gary Gygax.

FOLIE À DEUX: A form of psychosis where delusions—and, sometimes, full-out hallucinations—are actually shared between two or more individuals.

GAME MASTER: The designated person in charge of a campaign, who administers decisions as the game progresses.

GARY GYGAX: A famed game designer who cocreated Dungeons & Dragons with Dave Arneson and cofounded TSR (Tactical Studies Rules) Inc.

GUIDON GAMES: Founded in 1971, a company that heavily influenced the formation of TSR. The company put out Chainmail under the direction of Gary Gygax, who was one of their first employees. It was also where Gygax and Dave Arneson first collaborated on their first wargaming effort: Don't Give Up the Ship. Guidon Games was also one of the first companies that made use of a 20-sided die.

HAN DYNASTY: Spanning from 202 BCE–9 CE and again from 25–220 CE, an Imperial dynasty in ancient China, ruled by the House of Liu (descendants of Liu Bang).

THE HORN-BUTTING GAME: Part martial arts, part performance, this Han Dynasty performance positioned actors against each other to wrestle while dressed in thematic costumes to act out legends. These actors interacted with the audience, often utilizing props.

THE INTER-NATION SIMULATION:
Roleplaying statecraft games developed by two professors from Northwestern at the RAND Corporation in 1957. These games served to create and solve potential diplomatic and military problems in a safe and studied way.

JACOB LEVY MORENO: Born in 1889 in Bucharest, Romania, Moreno is known as the creator of drama therapy in the West, beginning with what he called "psychodrama."

JOHANN CHRISTIAN LUDWIG HELLWIG: A German entomologist, mathematics professor, and game designer who created an early version of Kriegsspiel in 1780.

THE JURY BOX: Released in 1937, a mashup of early board games meant to instruct and simulate a trial while incorporating roleplaying elements.

KRIEGSSPIEL: Developed by military personnel in nineteenth-century Prussia, Kriegsspiel are known as the first modern wargames. Though other games before it dealt with military concepts (such as Chaturanga and Chess), Kriegsspiel utilized realistic terrain and game pieces to recreate the theater of war on the tabletop for the purposes of simulating and teaching war strategy. These games, however, would soon become used for recreational purposes.

LARP: Short for Live Action Roleplaying, LARPing brings a player's character from a tabletop campaign into a simulation of real life. Players create costumes, (nonlethal) weaponry, and more. They then participate in simulated battles, exploration, encounters, and more.

LITTLE WARS: An anachronistic wargame created by the renowned science fiction writer HG Wells in 1913 that utilized highly detailed terrains and figurines, often painted by the player.

THE LORD OF THE RINGS: The seminal high-fantasy trilogy written by J.R.R. Tolkien, consisting of *The Fellowship of the Ring*, *The Two Towers*, and *The Return of the King*. This trilogy also heavily inspired the creation of Dungeons & Dragons.

THE MANSION OF HAPPINESS: Introduced to the US from Britain in 1802, but released later on in the United States in 1843, this game resembled the dynamics of Chutes and Ladders,

but with a series of perceived "good" and "evil" moral life developments.

MINI-FIGURINES: Figurines that can come either painted or unpainted (allowing the owner to paint the pieces themselves), and that can be used to facilitate gameplay—combat in particular—in tabletop gaming.

MR. REE!: THE FIRESIDE DETECTIVE: Created in 1937, this game bears resemblance to Clue, with added roleplaying elements, as players were asked to act out their roles.

NAPOLEONIC WARGAMERS (GROGNARDS): A name given to Napoleon's imperial guard that would come to refer to any wargamer with old-fashioned tastes.

NAUMACHIA: Referring to both the staging of naval battles and the basins or buildings themselves in the ancient Roman world.

NONPLAYER CHARACTER (NPC): A character that is actively controlled by the GM of a given game.

PATOLLI: A pre-Columbian game played in roughly 200 BCE across a variety of cultures throughout Mesoamerica, Patolli is a racing game with elements of wargaming attached, involving gambling and divine dictates.

PLAYER CHARACTER: A character that is actively controlled by a member of the gaming party.

POPE AND PAGAN: Published in the US in 1844, this game, made for Protestants, had mechanics structured around a "Christian Army" of missionaries whose goal was to lay siege to the "Stronghold of Satan."

PSYCHODRAMA: A form of therapy that uses self-presentation and dramatic performance—what Moreno referred to as roleplaying—in order to conduct improvised theater.

RAND CORPORATION: A research group founded in 1948 to serve the U.S. Military that utilized roleplaying games in an attempt to study and simulate real-world diplomacy and warfare, among a variety of other topics.

SAVING THROW: Originally featured in game designer Tony Bath's Rules for Medieval Wargames (1966), a saving throw is determined by rolling dice to determine the outcome of a character or monster's ability to be affected by an attack.

THE SOCIETY FOR CREATIVE ANACHRONISM: Founded by Diana Paxson, this group was Coventry's spiritual successor and has the aim of studying and recreating mainly Medieval European cultures and their histories before the seventeenth century.

STRATEGOS: A more modern wargame created for expressly military purposes by Charles Adiel Lewis Totten—an American military officer, professor, and writer—in 1880.

SWORD AND SORCERY: A genre coined by writer Fritz Leiber (Fafhrd and the Gray Mouser) to describe the early works of Robert E. Howard (of Conan the Barbarian fame), Sword and Sorcery often depicts morally ambiguous characters against each other in dark fantasy settings, without focusing on axioms of good and evil. Other examples of the Sword and Sorcery genre can be found in Michael Moorcock's Elric series, and more recently, Andrzej Sapkowski's The Witcher series.

TABLETOP ROLEPLAYING GAME (TTRPG): Games that combine statistics-based tactical gaming with interactive storytelling and improvisational theater.

TERRACOTTA WARRIORS: Terracotta figurines buried with Qin Shi Huang, the first emperor of China, in order to protect him in the afterlife. This massive figurine army was made up of thousands of soldiers and hundreds of chariots, cavalry, and horses.

THE TRAVELLERS' TOUR THROUGH THE UNITED STATES: Known as the first American board game when it debuted in 1822, players mapped their way through early American states and territories.

BIBLIOGRAPHY

BOOKS

Averbakh, Yuri, and Garry Kasparov. *A History of Chess: From Chaturanga to the Present Day*. Russell Enterprises, Inc, 2016.

Campbell, Joseph, and Bill Moyers. *The Power of Myth*. 1991.

Ewalt, David M. *Of Dice and Men: The Story of Dungeons & Dragons and the People Who Play It*. 2013.

Fine, Gary Alan. *Shared Fantasy: Role Playing Games as Social Worlds*. University of Chicago Press, 1983.

Jung, Carl. *The Archetypes and the Collective Unconscious*. Princeton University Press, 1969.

Mackerras, Colin. *Chinese Theater: From Its Origins to the Present Day*. University of Hawaii Press, 1988.

Miller, Carolyn Handler. *Digital Storytelling 4e: A Creator's Guide to Interactive Entertainment*. Routledge, 2014.

Peterson, Jon. *Playing at the World: A History of Simulating Wars, People, and Fantastic Adventures, from Chess to Role-Playing Games*. Unreason Press, 2012.

Yeung, Tuen Wai Mary. *To Entertain and Renew: Operas, Puppet Plays, and Ritual in South China*. Thesis for Doctor of Philosophy in the Faculty of Graduate Studies (Asian Studies), the University of British Columbia, Sept 2007.

Zagal, José P., and Sebastian Deterding. *Role-Playing Game Studies: Transmedia Foundations*. Routledge, 2018.

BOOK EXCERPTS & ACADEMIC ARTICLES

Roleplaying Games—Theory

Comeaux, Malcolm L. "What Games Can Say: Two Medieval Games from French Louisiana." *Louisiana History: The Journal of the Louisiana Historical Association* , vol. 46, no. 1 (2005): 47–63. www.jstor.org/stable/4234083.

Doty, Gene. "A Toss of the Dice: Writers, Readers, and Role-Playing Games." *Journal of the Fantastic in the Arts*, vol. 14, no. 1 (2003): 51–67. www.jstor.org/stable/43321454.

Ettkin, Larry, and Lester Snyder. "A Model for Peer Group Counseling Based on Role-Playing." *The School Counselor*, vol. 19, no. 3 (1972): 215–18. www.jstor.org/stable/23896717.

Ghamari-Tabrizi, Sharon. "Simulating the Unthinkable: Gaming Future War in the 1950s and 1960s." *Social Studies of Science*, vol. 30, no. 2 (2000): 163–223. www.jstor.org/stable/285834.

Glasberg, Davita Silfen, Barbara Nangle, Florence Maatita, and Tracy Schauer. "Games Children Play: An Exercise Illustrating Agents of Socialization." *Teaching Sociology*, vol. 26, no. 2 (1998): 130–39. www.jstor.org/stable/1319284.

Hammer, Jessica, and Drew Davidson. "Cultural Alignment and Game-Based Learning." *Educational Technology*, vol. 57, no. 2 (2017): 31–35. www.jstor.org/stable/44430521.

Howell, Maxwell L., Charles Dodge, and Reet A. Howell. "Generalizations On Play In 'Primitive' Societies." *Journal of Sport History*, vol. 2, no. 2 (1975): 145–55. www.jstor.org/stable/43611514.

Milspaw, Yvonne J., and Wesley K. Evans. "Variations on Vampires: Live Action Role Playing, Fantasy and the Revival of Traditional Beliefs." *Western Folklore*, vol. 69, no. 2 (2010): 211–50. www.jstor.org/stable/27896342.

O'Neill, Barb. "'There's a Crocodile!': Training Preschool Teachers to Engage Children through Interactive Oral Storytelling." *Storytelling, Self, Society*, vol. 11, no. 2 (2015): 183–210.

Owen, Lucia. "Dragons in the Classroom." *The English Journal*, vol. 73, no. 7 (1984): 76–77. www.jstor.org/stable/i233703.

Roberts, John M., Malcolm J. Arth, and Robert R. Bush. "Games in Culture." *American Anthropologist*. New Series, vol. 61, no. 4 (1959): 597–605. www.jstor.org/stable/667148.

Schlenker, Barry R., and Thomas V. Bonoma. "Fun and Games: The Validity of Games for the Study of Conflict." *The Journal of Conflict Resolution*, vol. 22, no. 1 (1978): 7–38. www.jstor.org/stable/173626.

Sutton-Smith, Brian. "Children's Folk Games as Customs." *Western Folklore*, vol. 48, no. 1 (1989): 33–42.

Uno, Tsunehiro, and translated by Jeffrey C. Guarneri. "Imagination after the Earthquake: Japan's Otaku Culture in the 2010s." *Verge: Studies in Global Asias*, vol. 1, no. 1 (2015): 114–36.

Patolli

Tylor, E. B. "On the Game of Patolli in Ancient Mexico, and Its Probably Asiatic Origin." *The Journal of the Anthropological Institute of Great Britain and Ireland*, vol. 8 (1879): 116–31.

Voorhies, Barbara. "The Deep Prehistory of Indian Gaming: Possible Late Archaic Period Game Boards at the Tlacuachero Shellmound, Chiapas, Mexico." *Latin American Antiquity*, vol. 24, no. 1 (2013): 98–115. www.jstor.org/stable/43746261.

Shadowplay, China, Theater

Becker, Glenn. *Theatre Journal* 50, no. 2 (1998): 282–83. www.jstor.org/stable/25068543. Reviewed Work: Inside the Drama-House: Rama Stories and Shadow Puppets in South India by Stuart Blackburn.

Børdahl, Vibeke. "The Man-Hunting Tiger: From 'Wu Song Fights the Tiger' in Chinese Traditions." *Asian Folklore Studies*, vol. 66, no. 1/2 (2007): 141–63. www.jstor.org/stable/30030454.

Conteh-Morgan, John. "African Traditional Drama and Issues in Theater and Performance Criticism." *Comparative Drama*, vol. 28, no. 1 (1994): 3–18.

Dolby, William. "The Origins of Chinese Puppetry." *Bulletin of the School of Oriental and African Studies, University of London*, vol. 41, no. 1 (1978): 97–120. JSTOR, www.jstor.org/stable/615625.

Jurkowski, Henryk. *Aspects of Puppet Theater*. Bloomsbury Publishing, 2014: 182–89.

McCurley, Dallas. "'Juedixi': An Entertainment of War in Early China." *Asian Theatre Journal*, vol. 22, no. 1 (2005): 87–106. JSTOR, www.jstor.org/stable/4137077.

Mori, Mitsuya. "The Structure of Theater: A Japanese View of Theatricality." *SubStance*, vol. 31, no. 2/3 (2002): 73–93.

Orr, Inge C. "Puppet Theatre in Asia." *Asian Folklore Studies*, vol. 33, no. 1 (1974): 69–84.

Özcan, Oğuzhan. "Cultures, the Traditional Shadow Play, and Interactive Media Design." *Design Issues*, vol. 18, no. 3 (2002): 18–26. www.jstor.org/stable/1512063.

Wan Nor Raihan Wan Ramli, and Farrah 'Aini Lugiman / Procedia. "The Contribution of Shadow Puppet's Show through Engaging Social Communication in Modern Society." *Social and Behavioral Sciences*, vol. 35 (2012): 353–60.

Jacob Moreno

Borgatta, Edgar F., Robert Boguslaw, and Martin R. Haskell. "On the Work of Jacob L. Moreno." *Sociometry*, vol. 38, no. 1 (1975): 148–61.

Howie, Peter C. "Philosophy of Life: J. L. Moreno's Revolutionary Philosophical Underpinnings of Psychodrama and Group Psychotherapy." *Group*, vol. 36, no. 2 (2012): 135–46. www.jstor.org/stable/41939407.

WEBSITES & ONLINE PDFs

Inter Nation Simulations/RAND

The Gaming of Policy and the Politics of Gaming—A Review (Subject: Simulation and Gaming since 1969): https://scienceimpact.mit.edu/sites/default/files/documents/The%20Gaming%20of%20Policy%20and%20the%20Politics%20of%20Gaming.pdf

INS (Inter Nation Simulation) Kit, 1969, Harold Gueztkow and Cleo H. Cherry Holmes; Northwestern University: http://www.ua69.com/PhotoCollections/SteveHolloway/InterNation/InterNation%20Simulation%20FullDocument.pdf

Pardee RAND Research Methods: https://www.prgs.edu/research/methods-centers/gaming.html

The Prisoner's Dilemma: https://en.wikipedia.org/wiki/Prisoner%27s_dilemma

RAND Corporation (Games of Strategy: Theory and Applications): https://www.rand.org/pubs/commercial_books/CB149-1.html

Coventry

Coventry (Fancyclopedia): http://fancyclopedia.org/Coventry

THEN by Rob Hansen—Chapter 9 (Fan Histories—Coventry): http://fanac.org/Fan_Histories/Then/Then_41.html

Domesday Book

Domesday Book: https://www.acaeum.com/library/domesday.html

Diplomacy

The Art of Negotiation in Diplomacy (Lewis Pulsipher): https://pulsiphergames.com/diplomacy/ArtofNegotiation.htm

Diplomacy (Board Game Geek): https://boardgamegeek.com/image/221306/diplomacy

The Diplomacy Archive: https://diplomacyzines.co.uk

Diplomacy Zines (Internet Archive): https://archive.org/details/diplomacyzines?&sort=-date&page=9

Fredonia Issue 11 (Diplomacy Fanzine, 1964): https://archive.org/details/Fredonia_11-17-1964/mode/2up

Gygax / D&D / Fantasy

Ability Checks—From the Worst Mechanic in Role-Playing Game History to a Foundation of D&D (DMDavid): https://dmdavid.com/tag/ability-checks-from-the-worst-mechanic-in-role-playing-game-history-to-a-foundation-of-dd/

Dragon Magazine #95, March, 1985 (Gary Gygax interview, pp. 14–15): https://archive.org/stream/DragonMagazine260_201801/DragonMagazine095#page/n13/mode/2up

Dungeons & Deceptions: The First D&D Players Push Back on the Legend of Gary Gygax (Kotaku): https://kotaku.com/dungeons-deceptions-the-first-d-d-players-push-back-1837516834

Dungeons & Dragons Reveals Plans for Better Representation and Inclusivity (CBR): https://www.cbr.com/dungeons-and-dragons-representation-inclusivity-plans/

D&D Will Change to Address Racism, But Someone Has Already Done the Work (Polygon): https://www.polygon.com/reviews/2020/7/9/21317614/dungeons-dragons-dnd-race-ancestry-and-culture-book?fbclid=IwAR2N6lxhbDKoiE5A4oK4X14JQ5jVX4MQ5ywk4fjcw27YfHvku0Ed3Pi_X3Y

For 25 Years, D&D Put Saving Throws in Groups Made for Just 3 Creatures and 2 Spells (DM David): https://dmdavid.com/tag/for-25-years-dd-put-saving-throws-in-groups-made-for-just-3-creatures-and-2-spells/

Hobbits and Hippies: Tolkien and the Counterculture (BBC): https://www.bbc.com/culture/article/20141120-the-hobbits-and-the-hippies

Playing at the World: History of D&D in 12 Treasures (Playing at the World blog): http://playingattheworld.blogspot.com/2014/01/history-of-d-in-12-treasures.html

Race: The Original Sin of the Fantasy Genre: https://www.publicmedievalist.com/race-fantasy-genre/

Should We Call Historians to Account for Distorting Arneson? (The Ruins of Murkhill forum): https://ruinsofmurkhill.proboards.com/thread/1440/call-historians-account-distorting-arneson

Tolkien and Dungeons & Dragons (The Artifice): https://the-artifice.com/tolkien-dungeons-dragons/

Commedia Dell'Arte

Acting Style in Commedia Dell'Arte: http://commedia.klingvall.com/commedia-dellarte/acting-style-in-commedia-dellarte/#:~:text=Since%20Commedia%20dell'Arte%20is,with%20acting%20with%20the%20audience

Commedia Dell'Arte (Britannica): https://www.britannica.com/art/commedia-dellarte

Commedia Dell'Arte (Metropolitan Museum of Art): https://www.metmuseum.org/toah/hd/comm/hd_comm.htm

Parlor Games

Before Monopoly All the Kids Were Wild about Pope and Pagan: https://www.newenglandhistoricalsociety.com/before-monopoly-all-the-kids-were-wild-about-pope-and-pagan/#:~:text=In%201844%2C%20young%20people%20of,Two%20players%20were%20needed

The Jury Box (Board Game Geek): https://boardgamegeek.com/image/3436486/jury-box

Long Before Professor Plum There Was Mr. Ree the Fireside Detective: https://stgrundyblog.wordpress.com/2016/12/29/long-before-professor-plum-there-was-mr-ree-the-fireside-detective/

Chainmail / Blackmoor / Medieval

The "Blackmoor Is Just a Chainmail Variant" Fallacy (Havard's Blackmoor Blog): http://blackmoormystara.blogspot.com/2016/03/the-blackmoor-is-just-chainmail-variant.html

Castle Blackmoor model and Jack Scruby Miniatures: https://www.reddit.com/r/odnd/comments/c0cdr1/blackmoor_castle_blackmoor_model_and_jack_scruby/

Chainmail Alignment Chart (Grognardia): http://grognardia.blogspot.com/2012/07/chainmail-alignment-chart.html

Dave Arneson's Blackmoor Character Record Sheet: https://boardgamegeek.com/forum/2362657/dave-arnesons-blackmoor-character-record-sheet/rules

Secrets of Blackmoor: A D&D Documentary: www.secretsofblackmoor.com

The Tangled Origins of D&D's Armor Class, Hit Points, and Twenty-Sided Die Rolls To-Hit (DMDavid): https://dmdavid.com/tag/the-tangled-origins-of-dds-armor-class-hit-points-and-twenty-sided-die-rolls-to-hit/#:~:text=Poster%20Maps-,The%20Tangled%20Origins%20of%20D%26D's%20Armor%20Class%2C%20Hit%20Points%2C%20and,Sided%20Die%20Rolls%20To-Hit&text=Chainmail%20rated%20armor%20from%201,His%20campaign%20developed%20into%20D%26D

Tolkien Board Games - Chainmail: https://tolkienvisualcollectingguide.blogspot.com/2020/06/tolkien-early-board-games.html

Wargaming

Game Studies: Notes from the Wargaming Underground: Dungeons, Dragons, and the History of Games (gamestudies.org): http://gamestudies.org/1302/articles/trammell

Kriegspiel (Board Game Geek): https://boardgamegeek.com/image/252855/kriegspiel

Kriegspiel (r-s-g.org): http://r-s-g.org/kriegspiel/about.php

Kriegsspiel—Rules and Playing Aids (Kriegsspielorg): https://kriegsspielorg.wordpress.com/resources-2/rules-and-playing-aids/

Nineteenth Century Military War Games: Lieutenant von Reisswitz's Kriegsspiel (Grogheads): https://edmwargamemeanderings.blogspot.com/2019/05/von-reisswitz-kriegspiel-shooting-some.html

A Short History of Wargaming by Brendan Courtsal: https://prezi.com/8wgbczjjetam/a-short-history-of-wargaming/

The Von Reisswitz Kriegsspiel: The Prussian Army Wargame (BoardGameGeek): https://boardgamegeek.com/boardgame/16957/von-reisswitz-kriegsspiel-prussian-army-wargame

Chinese Theater/Puppetry

Called "Marionette Show" in Ancient China, a Puppet Show Is a Theatre Performance: https://resources.made-in-china.com/article/culture-life/NQEmdWTrVxIb/Puppet-Shows/

China Fact Tours (Chinese Shadow Puppet Show): http://www.chinafacttours.com/facts/art/chinese-piying-show.html

Chinese Performing Arts (Encyclopedia Britannica): https://www.britannica.com/art/Chinese-performing-arts

Dragon Dance during the Han Dynasty: https://www.wikiwand.com/en/Dragon_dance

The Early History of Chinese Theater: https://disco.teak.fi/asia/the-early-history-of-chinese-theatre/

Funeral banner of Lad Dai (Khan Academy): https://www.khanacademy.org/humanities/ap-art-history/south-east-se-asia/china-art/a/funeral-banner-of-lady-dai-xin-zhui

The Great General Han Xin (Shenyun Performing Arts): https://www.shenyunperformingarts.org/explore/view/article/e/JfGGykaiFjY/han-xin-chinese-stories-history.html

Jiaodi (An Ancient Wrestling Skill): http://en.chinaculture.org/library/2008-01/23/content_37734.htm

The Magic of Chinese Theatre: Theatre as a Rritualo of Sacral Transmogrification, by Margaret Chan, Singapore Management University: https://ink.library.smu.edu.sg/soss_research/713/

Master Puppeteer Gives Ancient Chinese Art a 21st Century Update: https://zolimacitymag.com/a-master-puppeteer-gives-an-ancient-chinese-art-a-21st-century-update/

Nuo Culture (ChinaCulture.org): http://en.chinaculture.org/created/2005-12/08/content_76926.htm

Puppetry in China (Youlin Magazine): https://www.youlinmagazine.com/article/puppetry-in-china/MTc1MA==

World Encyclopedia of Puppetry Arts—Puppetry in China: https://wepa.unima.org/en/china/

Naumachiae

Aqua Clopedia, a picture dictionary Roman Aqueducts: Naumachia: http://www.romanaqueducts.info/picturedictionary/pd_onderwerpen/naumachia.htm

Gladiators of the Sea (Slate): https://slate.com/human-interest/2016/01/the-roman-naumachiae-water-battles-that-forced-prisoners-to-re-enact-naval-campaigns-to-entertain-emperors.html

The Naumachia of Titus and Domitian in the Colosseum (UChicago.edu): https://penelope.uchicago.edu/~grout/encyclopaedia_romana/gladiators/naumachiae.html

Why Ancient Rome Staged Epic, Violent Sea Battles (National Geographic): https://www.nationalgeographic.com/history/magazine/2017/09-10/roman-mock-naval-sea-battles-naumachia/

Jacob Moreno

The Cosmo-Theological Concepts of Jacob L. Moreno: Universal Spontaneity-Creativity (Paper Presented at the Sixth International Congress in Psychodrama and Sociodrama in Amsterdam, Holland, 1971), by Robert T. Sears, SJ, PhD: http://www.familytreehealing.com/J%20L%20Moreno%20paper%20final%20edit%20for%20JCH%2011-21-17.pdf

Moreno Museum: http://www.moreno-museum.at/moreno-museum-biography-en.html

Chaturanga & Chess

Chaturanga (Cyngistan): http://www.cyningstan.com/game/1454/chaturanga

Chaturanga for Four Players (The Chess Variant): https://www.chessvariants.com/historic.dir/chaturang4.html

Chess (Encyclopaedia Iranica): https://iranicaonline.org/articles/chess-a-board-game

Chess—History (Britannica): https://www.britannica.com/topic/chess/History

From Chaturanga to Chess—The History of the Origin of Chess (Home Grown): https://homegrown.co.in/article/803547/from-chaturanga-to-chess-the-history-of-the-origin-of-chess

On the origins of chess (ChessBase): https://en.chessbase.com/post/on-the-origins-of-chess-1-5

Origins of chess (chess.com): https://www.chess.com/article/view/origins-of-chess#:~:text=In%20 1005%20al%2Dhakim%20of,the%20Conqueror%20was%20playing%20chess

Where Did Chess Originate (World Atlas): https://www.worldatlas.com/articles/where-did-chess-originate.html

Board Games

Mr. Ree Fireside Detective Game:
https://boardgamegeek.com/boardgame/2924/mr-ree-fireside-detective
https://stgrundyblog.wordpress.com/2016/12/29/long-before-professor-plum-there-was-mr-ree-the-fireside-detective/

Mystery Games: https://thebiggamehunter.com/collecting/themes/mystery-games/

Pre-Modern American Board and Card Games: https://artsandculture.google.com/exhibit/american-board-and-card-game-history/9wJiZCrQ9FmHJw

Roleplaying Games—Theory

Making Meaningful Worlds: Role-playing Subcultures and the Autism Spectrum Cult Med Psychiatry. 2015 Jun; 39(2): 299–321.doi: 10.1007/s11013-015-9443-x

ABOUT THE AUTHORS

Photo courtesy of the author

STEENZ is a St. Louis, Missouri–based cartoonist, editor, and professor. They are the cartoonist on the Ringo Award–nominated and syndicated comic strip *Heart of the City*, the cocreator of the Dwayne McDuffie Award–winning graphic novel *Archival Quality*, and the cocreator of the Standard Comic Script. Steenz currently teaches at Webster University and School of Visual Arts while editing titles from independent publishers and creators. They are also board president of SLICE (the St. Louis Independent Comics Expo).

Author photo by Grace Harper

SAMUEL SATTIN is an American writer. His books include the multivolume Unico series, *Buzzing*, and (as coauthor) both *A Kid's Guide to Anime and Manga* and *The Essential Anime Guide: 50 Iconic Films, Standout Series, and Cult Masterpieces*. He has also adapted the Academy Award–nominated films *WolfWalkers*, *Song of the Sea*, and *The Secret of Kells* to the graphic novel format. He graduated with an MFA in comics from the California College of the Arts and works as a studio writer for Schulz Creative Associates, a.k.a. Snoopy Central. Samuel resides with his wife in San Francisco, California.